ALL HA

SATA
ZIONIST
LUCIFERIAN
NECROMANTIC

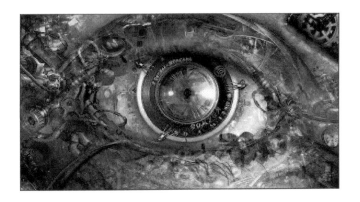

MASONIC
JESUIT
CIA
MAFIA
SHADOW
GOVERNMENT
ELITE
ESTABLISHMENT

C000059553

JOSEF ROTHSCHILD
& HIS CHILDREN

ILLUMINATI

BASED ON THE TEXT BY

MYRON FAGAN

A DISTANT MIRROR

Based on the 1967 recordings by Myron Fagan.

PRINT ISBN 979-8-6543879-6-7

EPUB ISBN 978-1-3659793-5-4

Every effort has been made to identify and contact potential copyright holders of the images used in this book.

Published by

📍 ADISTANTMIRROR.COM

✉ ADMIN@ADISTANTMIRROR.COM

MYRON FAGAN

INTRODUCTION

THE PUBLICATION *Who's Who in the Theater* never played favorites, it told no lies, it glorified nobody. It always was an unbiased history of the men and women in the theater. It recorded only those who proved their worth in the leading testing place of the theater, Broadway. *Who's Who in the Theater* records the plays that Myron C. Fagan wrote, directed and produced: dramas, comedies, melodramas, mysteries, allegories, and farces. Many of them were resounding hits.

He arrived on Broadway in 1907, 19 years old, the youngest playwright in the history of the American theater. In the following years, he wrote and directed plays for many of the greats of those days, including Mrs Leslie Carter, Wilton Lackaye, Fritz Leiber, Alla Nazimova, Jack Barrymore, Douglas Fairbanks Sr., E.H. Southern, Julia Marlowe, and Helen Morgan.

He directed Charles M. Frohman, Belasco, Henry W. Savage, Lee Shubert, Abe Erlanger, and George M. Cohan, among others.

In the five years between 1925 and 1930 he wrote, directed, and produced twelve plays: *The White Rose, Thumbs Down, Two Strangers from Nowhere, Mismates, The Fascinating Devil, The Little Spitfire, Jimmy's Women, The Great Power, Indiscretion, Nancy's Private Affair, Smart Woman,* and *Peter Flies High.*

During his early years, Myron Fagan was also dramatic editor for Associated Newspapers, including *The New York Globe,* as well as and various Hearst newspapers.

In 1916 he took a sabbatical from the theater and served as director of public relations for Charles Hughes, the Republican candidate for the Presidency. He refused a similar post offered to him in the Herbert Hoover campaign in 1928.

Mr. Fagan's career encompassed the theater, journalism, and national politics. He was proven to be capable in all those fields.

In 1930, Fagan came to Hollywood, where he served as writer and director with Pathe Pictures, then owned by Joseph P. Kennedy, father of the late President Jack Kennedy, and also at 20th Century Fox, and other Hollywood film studios; but he also continued in Broadway.

In 1945, at the urgent request of John T. Flynn (the famous author of *The Roosevelt Myth*, *While We Slept*, and *The True Story of Pearl Harbor*), Mr. Fagan attended a meeting in Washington D.C. where he was shown a set of micro-films and recordings of the secret meetings at Yalta attended only by Franklin Roosevelt, Alger Hess, Harry Hopkins, Stalin, Molotov, and Vishinsky, when they hatched the plot to deliver the Balkans, Eastern Europe and Berlin to Stalin.

As a result of that viewing, Fagan wrote two plays; *Red Rainbow* (in which he revealed that entire plot) and *Thieves' Paradise* (in which he revealed how those men plotted to create the United Nations to be the vehicle for a communist world government).

At the same time, Mr. Fagan launched a one man crusade to unmask the Red conspiracy in Hollywood which had set about to produce films that aimed to spread and support the plot to establish a world government.

Out of that came into being the Cinema Educational Guild. As a result of the work of the CEG (which was headed by Fagan) in 1947 came the congressional hearings at which more than

I HAZ SEEN WAT IZ IN DA BOX

DA ILLUMINATI MUS NEVER LEARN OF DIS

300 famous stars, writers, and directors from Hollywood, radio, and television were unmasked as the chief activists of the Red conspiracy. That was when the infamous 'Hollywood Ten' were sent to prison. It was the most sensational event of the decade.

From that time on, Mr. Fagan devoted all of his time and efforts to writing monthly news bulletins for CEG, in which he kept up the fight to alert the American people to the plot to destroy the sovereignty of the United States of America, and bring about the ensuing enslavement of the American people under a United Nations' world government.

In his recording *The Illuminati and The Council on Foreign Relations* (the transcript of which is the foundation of this book), he reveals the beginning of the 'One World' enslavement plot that was launched two centuries ago by Adam Weishaupt, an apostate Catholic priest who, financed and supported by the House of Rothchild, created the organisation which Weishaupt called the 'Illuminati', and which we now describe with many different names.

Fagan describes how the Illuminati became the instrument of the Rothschild plan to establish a world government, and how every war during the past two centuries has been fomented by this Illuminati.

He describes how Jacob Schiff was sent to the United States

IF YOU CAN POKE ROYALTY ON THEIR CHEST LIKE THEY'RE YOUR BITCH

YOU MAY BE A ROTHSCHILD

by the Rothschilds to further the Illuminati plot and how Schiff plotted to get control of both the Democratic and Republican parties. He shows how Schiff seduced our Congress and our Presidents, to achieve control of our entire money system and create the income tax, and how Schiff and his co-conspirators created the Council on Foreign Relations to control our elected officials to gradually drive the U.S. into becoming part of a United Nations world government.

In short, Fagan's words form a horrifying—and factual—story of what is perhaps the most sensational plot in the history of the world.

ILLUMINATI

"Hello there.

My name is Jacob Rothschild.

My family is worth 500 trillion dollars.

We own almost every central bank in the world.

We have financed both sides of every war
since the time of Napoleon.

We own your news, your media,
your oil, and your government.

You have probably never heard of me."

THE QUESTION of how and why the United Nations is the crux of the great conspiracy to destroy the sovereignty of the United States and the enslavement of the American people within a U.N. world dictatorship is a complete and unknown mystery to the vast majority of the American people.

The reason for this lack of awareness of the frightening danger to our country and to the entire free world is simple. The masterminds behind this great conspiracy have absolute control over all of our mass media – especially television, radio, the press, and Hollywood.

We all know that our State Department, the Pentagon, and the White House have brazenly proclaimed that they have the right and the power to manage the news, and to tell us not the truth, but what they want us to believe. They have seized that power on orders from the masters of the great conspiracy, and the objective is to brainwash the people into accepting the phoney peace bait; to transform the United States into an enslaved unit of the United Nations' world government.

First of all, bear in mind that the so-called U.N. 'police action' in Korea, in which 150,000 of our sons were murdered and maimed, was part of the plot; just as the undeclared-by-Congress war in Vietnam in which our sons are dying now is part of the plot.

ADAM WEISHAUPT

However, the vitally important thing for all Americans to know, all you mothers of the boys who died in Korea and are now dying in Vietnam – is that our so-called leaders in Washington, who we elected to safeguard our nation and our Constitution, are traitors, and that behind them are a comparatively small group of men whose sole objective is to enslave the whole world of humanity in their satanic plot to establish a world government.

Now, in order to give you a very clear picture of this conspiracy, I will go back to its beginning – to the middle of the 18th century – and introduce to you the men who put that plot into action, and then we will travel to the present, to the current status of the plot.

Now as a matter of 'further intelligence' (a term used by the FBI), let me clarify the meaning of the term 'liberal'. The enemy, meaning the one-world conspirators, have seized upon the word 'liberal' as a cover for their activities. It sounds so innocent and so humanitarian to be 'liberal'! Well, make sure that the person who calls himself a liberal, or is described by others as a liberal, is not in reality a Marxist.

Now then, this satanic plot was launched back in the 1760s when it first came into existence under the name 'Illuminati'. This group was organized by one Adam Weishaupt, a Jew who converted to Catholicism and became a Catholic priest, and then, at the behest of the House of Rothschild, defected and organized the Illuminati.

Naturally, the Rothschilds financed that operation, and every war since then, beginning with the French Revolution, has been promoted by the Illuminati operating under various names and guises. I say under various names and guises because after the Illuminati was exposed and became notorious, Weishaupt and his fellow conspirators began to operate under various other names.

In the United States, immediately after World War I, they set up what they called the *Council on Foreign Relations*, commonly referred to as the CFR.

This CFR is actually the Illuminati in the United States. The masterminds in control of the original Illuminati conspirators were foreigners. To conceal that fact, most of them changed their original family names to American-

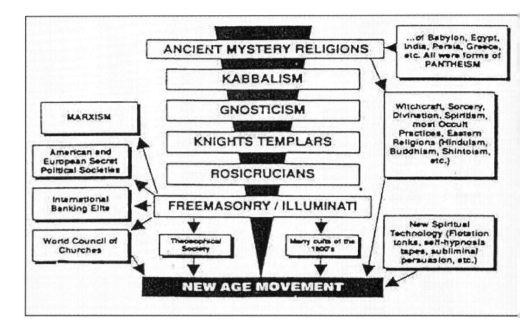

sounding names. For example, the true name of the Dillons –
Clarence and Douglas (one Secretary of the U.S. Treasury
Department) – is Laposky. I'll come back to this later.

There is a similar establishment of the Illuminati in
England, operating under the name of the *Royal Institute of
International Affairs*. There are also secret Illuminati
organizations in France, Germany, and other nations,
operating under different names.

All these organizations, including the CFR, set up
numerous subsidiary or front organizations that are
infiltrated into every phase of the various nations' affairs.

At all times, the operations of these organizations were
and are masterminded and controlled by the internationalist
bankers, and they in turn were and are controlled by the
Rothschilds.

One of the prime agents in this control is through the

"I care not what puppet is placed upon the throne of England to rule the Empire on which the sun never sets. The man who controls Britain's money supply controls the British Empire, and I control the British money supply."

– *Nathan Rothschild*

International Bar Association and its splinter groups such as the American Bar Association. There are Bar Associations in nearly every nation world wide, pushing the U.N.

One branch of the Rothschild family financed Napoleon; another branch of the family financed Britain, Germany, and the other nations during the Napoleonic wars.

Immediately after the Napoleonic wars, the Illuminati assumed that all the nations were so destitute and so weary of wars that they would be glad for any solution, so the Rothschild stooges set up what they called the Congress of Vienna, and at that meeting they tried to create the first League of Nations, their first attempted one world government, on the theory that all the crowned heads of European governments were so deeply in debt to them that they would willingly or unwillingly serve as their stooges.

CZAR ALEXANDER 1ˢᵗ OF RUSSIA

But the Czar of Russia caught the stench of the plot and completely torpedoed it. The enraged Nathan Rothschild, then the head of the dynasty, vowed that some day he or his descendants would destroy the Czar and his entire family. His descendants did accomplish that very threat in 1917.

At this point, bear in mind that the Illuminati was not set up to operate on a short term basis.

Normally a conspirator of any type enters into a conspiracy with the expectation of achieving his objective during his own lifetime.

But that was not the case with the Illuminati. True, they hoped to accomplish their objective during their lifetime, but "the show must go on", and the Illuminati operates on a long term basis.

Whether it will take scores of years or even centuries, they have committed their descendants to keeping the pot boiling until their goals are achieved.

Now, let's go back to the birth of the Illuminati.

ADAM WEISHAUPT was a Jesuit-trained professor of canon law, teaching in Engelstock University, when he defected from Christianity to embrace the Luciferian conspiracy.

It was in 1770 that the professional money lenders, the then recently organized House of Rothschild, retained him to revise and modernize the age-old protocols of Zionism, which from the outset, was designed to give the 'Synagogue of Satan,' so-named by Jesus Christ (and who are "them which say they are Jews and are not" – *Revelation 2:9*), total world domination so that they could impose their luciferian ideology upon what would

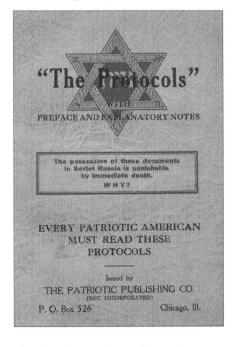

remain of the human race after the final cataclysm brought about through their use of Satanic despotism.

Weishaupt completed his task on May 1, 1776. Which is why May 1 is such a great day for all communist nations.

May 1 is also 'Law Day', according to the American Bar Association.

The celebration of May 1 (Baal/Beltane) goes much further back into history than this. The day was picked for ancient reasons, which come from the pagan worship of Baal and Satan.

That was the day, May 1, 1776, that Weishaupt completed his plan and officially created the Illuminati.

Weishaupt's plan called for the destruction of all governments and religions.

That objective was to be achieved by dividing the masses of people, who Weishaupt called *goyem* (nations), or human cattle, into opposing camps on political, social, economic, and other issues in ever-increasing numbers. These are the very conditions we have in our country today.

The opposing sides were

then to be armed, and incidents provided which would cause them to fight and weaken themselves, and gradually destroy national governments and religious institutions.

Again I say, these very conditions exist in the world today.

And now, let me outline a primary feature of the Illuminati plans.

When and if their blueprint for world control, *The Protocols of the Elders of Zion*, is discovered and exposed, they would wipe all the Jews off the face of the earth in order to divert suspicions from themselves.

If you think this is far fetched, bear in mind that they permitted Hitler, a liberal socialist, and who was financed by corrupt Kennedies, the Warburgs, and the Rothschilds, to incinerate the Jews.

Now just why did the conspirators choose the word *Illuminati* as the name for their satanic organization?

Weishaupt himself said that the word is derived from 'Lucifer' and means 'holder of the light'. He said this even as he told the world that his objective was to bring about a one world government to enable those with mental ability to govern the world, and prevent all wars in the future.

In short, using the words 'peace on earth' as his bait (exactly as the same idea of 'peace' was used by the 1945 conspirators to force the United Nations on us), Weishaupt,

Lucifer, Angel of Light 3 ☠ ☠ ☠

Legendary Creature — Angel

Fear, Flying, Indestructible

3 ☠ ☠ : Gain control of target creature an opponent controls, when that creature would leave the battlefield exile it instead.

When Lucifer, Angel of Light enters the battlefield exile three target creatures, at the beginning of your upkeep put one creature exiled this way on to the your side of the field at random.

7/6

financed by the Rothschilds, recruited some two thousand paid followers.

These included the most intelligent men in the field of arts and letters, education, the sciences, finance, and industry.

He then established Lodges of the Grand Orient, Masonic lodges to be their secret headquarters. In all of this he was acting under orders from the House of Rothschild.

The plan required his Illuminati to use monetary and sexual bribery to obtain control over people in high places in the various levels of government and other fields of endeavor.

Once influential people had fallen for the lies, deceits, and temptations, they were to be held in bondage by application of political and other forms of blackmail – threats of financial ruin, public exposure, and fiscal harm, even death to themselves and members of their families.

Do you realize how many top officials in our present government in Washington are controlled in just that way? Do you realize how many in our State Department, the Pentagon, all federal agencies, even in the White House, are controlled that way?

Illuminati agents in the faculties of colleges and universities were to cultivate students possessing exceptional mental ability belonging to well-bred families with international leanings, and recommend them for special training in internationalism. Such training was to be provided by granting scholarships to those selected by the Illuminatists.

That gives you an idea what a 'Rhodes Scholarship' means. It means indoctrination into the idea that only a one-world government can put an end to recurring wars and strife. That is how the United Nations was sold to the American people.

All such scholars were to be persuaded and convinced that people of special talent and brains have the right to rule those less gifted, on the grounds that the masses don't know what is best for them – fiscally, mentally, or spiritually.

In addition to the Rhodes and similar scholarships, today there are three special

Six Illuminati Media Corporations Own All Media Outlets .. ALL

GE	News Corp	Disney	Viacom	Time Warner	CBS
Comcast	FOX	ABC	Paramount	TWC	Showtime
NBC / CNBC	WSJ	A&E	MTV	AOL	The Movie Ch
Universal	New York Post	History	VH1	HBO	TV Guide
Pictures /	Barron's	H2	Neckelodeon	Cinemax	Smithonian Cl
Studios	Zondervan Pub	Bio.	Nick	Time Inc.	Simon & Shust
RCA	HarperCollins	Lifetime	United Int'l	CNN	FLIX
Weather	The Sun (UK)	ESPN	LOGO	Money Mag	CNET
Channel	The Daily	PIXAR	BET	Fortune Mag	NFL.com
Telemundo	Telegraph (UK)	MIRAMAX	CMT	People Mag	Westinghouse
more ...	AU News Corp	Marvel Ent	more ...	Golf Mag	Elctric Corp
	more ..	more ...		more ...	more ...

Illuminati schools located in Gordonstown in Scotland, Salem in Germany, and Annavrighta in Greece. These three are the known ones, but there are others that are kept undercover.

Prince Philip, the husband of Britain's Queen Elizabeth, was educated at Gordonstown (as also was Prince Charles) at the instigation of Lord Louis Mountbatten, his uncle, a Rothschild relative, who became Britain's Admiral of the Fleet after World War II ended.

All influential people who came under the control of the Illuminati, plus the students who had been specially educated and trained, were to be used as agents and placed behind the scenes of all governments as experts and specialists, so they would advise the top executives to adopt policies which would, in the long run, serve the plans of the Illuminati and

bring about the destruction of the governments and religions they were elected or appointed to serve.

Do you know how many such people operate in our government at this very time? Rusk, McNamara, Hubert Humphrey, Fulbright, Keekle – and the list goes on and on and on.

Perhaps the most vital part of Weishaupt's plan was the directive to obtain absolute control of the press (which at that time was the only mass media), to distribute information to the public so that all news and information could be slanted so that the masses could be convinced that a world government is the only solution to our many and varied problems.

Do you know who owns and controls our mass media? I'll

tell you. Practically all the movie lots in Hollywood are owned by the Lehmans, Goldman-Sachs, Kuhn, Loeb, and Company, and other internationalist bankers.

All the major radio and TV channels in the nation are owned and controlled by those same internationalist bankers. The same is true of every chain of metropolitan newspapers and magazines, also of the press wire services such as Associated Press, United Press, International, etc. The supposed heads of all those media are merely the fronts for the internationalist bankers, who in turn compose the hierarchy of the CFR, today's Illuminati in America.

Now can you understand why the Pentagon Press agent, Sylvester, so brazenly proclaimed that the government has the right to lie to the people. What he really meant was that our CFR-controlled government has the power to lie to – and be believed by – the brain-washed majority of the American people.

Nachtrag

von weitern

Originalschriften,

welche die

Illuminatensekte

überhaupt,

sonderbar aber den

Stifter derselben

Adam Weishaupt,

gewesenen Professor zu Ingolstadt

betreffen,

und

bey der auf dem Baron Bassusischen Schloß

zu Sandersdorf,

einem bekannten Illuminaten - Neste,

vorgenommenen Visitation entdeckt,

sofort auf

Churfürstlich höchsten Befehl

gedruckt,

und zum geheimen Archiv genommen worden

sind, um solche jedermann auf Verlangen

zur Einsicht vorlegen zu lassen.

Zwo Abtheilungen.

München, 1787.

LET US AGAIN go back to the first days of the Illuminati.

Because Britain and France were the two greatest world powers in the late years of the 18th Century, Weishaupt ordered the Illuminati to foment the colonial wars, including our Revolutionary War, to weaken the British Empire and organize the French Revolution to start in 1789.

However, in 1784, a true act of God placed the Bavarian

The Steps of Freemasonry

SCOTTISH RITE

25° Kn... the S...
24° Prince of the Tabernacle
23° Chief of the Tabernacle
22° Prince of Libanus
21° Patriarch Noachite
20° Master Ad Vitam
19° Grand Pontiff
18° Knight of the Rose Croix
17° Knight of the East and West
16° Prince of Jerusalem
15° Knight of the East or Sword
14° Grand Elect Mason
13° Master of the Ninth Arch
12° Grand Master Architect
11° Sublime Master Elected
10° Elect of Fifteen
9° Master Elect of Nine
8° Intendant of the Building
7° Provost and Judge
6° Intimate Secretary
5° Perfect Master
4° Secret Master

government in possession of evidence which proved the existence of the Illuminati. That evidence could have saved France, if the French government had only believed it.

Here is what happened.

It was in 1784 that Weishaupt issued his orders for the French Revolution. A German writer named Zweig put it into book form. It contained the entire Illuminati story and Weishaupt's plans.

A copy of this book was sent to the Illuminists in France headed by Robespierre, whom Weishaupt had delegated to foment the French Revolution. However, the courier was struck and killed by lightening as he rode through Rawleston, on his way from Frankfurt to Paris.

The police found the subversive documents on his body and turned them over to the proper authorities. After a careful study of the plot, the Bavarian government ordered the police to raid Weishaupt's newly organized 'Lodges of the Grand Orient' and the homes of his most influential associates.

All the evidence discovered convinced the authorities that the documents were genuine copies of the conspiracy by which the Illuminati planned to use wars and revolutions to bring about the establishment of a one-world government; the powers of which they, headed by the Rothschilds, intended to usurp as soon as it was established – exactly in line with the United Nations plot of today.

In 1785, the Bavarian government outlawed the Illuminati and closed the Lodges of the Grand Orient.

In 1786 they published all the details of the conspiracy. The English title of that publication is *The Original Writings of the Order and the Sect of the Illuminati.*

JOHN ROBISON

Copies of the entire conspiracy were sent to all the heads of church and state in Europe. But the power of the Illuminati – which was actually the power of the Rothschilds – was so great that this warning was ignored.

Nevertheless, the Illuminati became a dirty word, and it went underground.

At the same time, Weishaupt ordered his Illuminists to infiltrate into the 'Lodges of Blue Masonry'. Only Masons who proved themselves internationalists and whose conduct proved that they had defected from God were initiated into the Illuminati.

Thenceforth the conspirators donned the cloak of philanthropy and humanitarianism to conceal their subversive activities.

In order to infiltrate into Masonic Lodges in Britain, Weishaupt invited John Robison over to Europe. Robison was a high-degree Mason in the 'Scottish Rite'. He was a professor of natural philosophy at Edinburgh University and Secretary of the Royal Society of Edinburgh.

Robison did not fall for the lie that the objective of the Illuminati was to create a benevolent dictatorship; but he kept his thoughts to himself so well that he was entrusted with a copy of Weishaupt's revised conspiracy for study and safekeeping.

Because the heads of state and church in France were deluded into ignoring the warnings given to them, the revolution broke out in 1789 as scheduled by Weishaupt.

In order to alert other governments to the danger, in 1798 Robison published a book entitled *Proof of a Conspiracy to Destroy all Governments and Religions*, but his warnings were ignored, exactly as our American people have been ignoring all warnings about the United Nations and the Council on Foreign Relations.

ALEXANDER HAMILTON & THOMAS JEFFERSON

Now, here is something that will stun and very likely outrage many who read this: there is documentary proof that our own Thomas Jefferson and Alexander Hamilton became students of Weishaupt.

Jefferson was one of Weishaupt's strongest defenders when he was outlawed by his government, and it was Jefferson who infiltrated the Illuminati into the then newly-organized lodges of the 'Scottish Rite' in New England.

Here is the proof.

In 1789 John Robison warned all Masonic leaders in America that the Illuminati had infiltrated into their lodges.

On July 19, 1789 David Papen, President of Harvard University, issued the same warning to the graduating class, and lectured them on the influence that Illuminism was acquiring on American politics and religion.

To top it off, John Quincy Adams, who had organized the New England Masonic lodges, issued his own warnings. He wrote three letters to Colonel William Stone, a top Mason, in which he exposed how Jefferson was using Masonic lodges for subversive Illuministic purposes. Those three letters are at this very time in Whittenburg Square Library in Philadelphia.

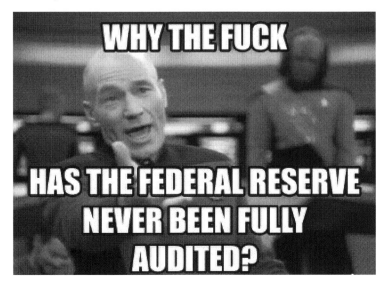

In short; Jefferson, founder of the Democratic Party, was a member of the Illuminati – which at least partly accounts for the condition of the party at this time. And with the infiltration of the Republican Party, we have exactly nothing of loyal Americanism today.

That disastrous rebuff at the Congress of Vienna by the Czar of Russia did not by any means destroy the Illuminati conspiracy. It merely forced them to adopt a new strategy acknowledging that the one-world idea was, for the moment, not feasible. The Rothschilds decided that to keep the plot alive, they would have to do it by strengthening their control over the financial systems of the European nations.

Earlier, in a massive deception, the outcome of the Battle of Waterloo had been falsified. Rothschild had spread a story that Napoleon had won, which precipitated a terrific panic on the stock-market in England. All stocks had plummeted down to practically zero, and Nathan Rothschild bought everything for a fraction of their normal values.

That gave him complete control of the economy of Britain and virtually of all Europe.

So, immediately after that Congress in Vienna had boomeranged, the Rothschilds had forced Britain to set up a new 'Bank of England', over which he had absolute control – exactly as later, through Jacob Schiff, they engineered our own *Federal Reserve Act*, which gave the House of Rothschild control of the economy in the United States.

Now, for a moment, let us dwell on the activities of the Illuminati in the United States.

William Morgan writing *Illustrations of Masonry*
(Anti-Masonic Almanac, 1829)

In 1826, one Captain William Morgan decided it was his duty to inform all Masons,, as well as the general public, of the full proof regarding the Illuminati – their secret plans and objectives – and to reveal the identities of the masterminds of the conspiracy.

The Illuminati promptly tried Morgan in absentia, and convicted him of treason. They ordered one Richard Howard, an English Illuminist, to carry out the sentence of execution. Morgan was warned and he tried to escape to Canada, but Howard caught up with him near the border – near the Niagara Gorge to be exact – where he murdered Morgan.

This was verified in a sworn statement made in New York by one Avery Allen, to the effect that he heard Howard render his report of the execution to a meeting of Knights Templars in New York. He also told how arrangements had been made to ship Howard back to England. That affidavit by Allen is on record in New York's city archives.

Very few Masons and very few of the general public know that general disapproval over Morgan's murder caused approximately half of all the Masons in the northern jurisdiction of the United States to secede. Copies of the minutes of the meeting held to discuss the matter are still in

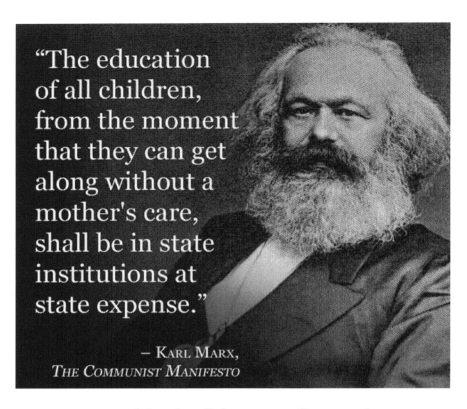

"The education of all children, from the moment that they can get along without a mother's care, shall be in state institutions at state expense."

— KARL MARX,
THE COMMUNIST MANIFESTO

existence in safe hands. All that secrecy illustrates the power of the masterminds of the Illuminati to prevent such historical events from being taught in our schools.

In the early 1850s, the Illuminati held a secret meeting in New York which was addressed by a British Illuminist named Wright. Those in attendance were told that the Illuminati was organizing to unite nihilist and atheist groups with other subversive groups, into an international movement to be known as 'communists'.

That was when the word *communist* first came into being, and it was intended to be the supreme weapon and scare word to terrify the whole world and drive the terrorized peoples into the Illuminati one-world scheme.

Communism was to be used to enable the Illuminati to instigate future wars and revolutions. Clinton Roosevelt, a direct ancestor of Franklin Roosevelt, and Horace Greeley and Charles Dana, newspaper publishers of that time, were appointed to head a committee to raise funds for the new venture. Of course, most of the funds were provided by the Rothschilds, and this fund was used to finance Karl Marx and Engels when they wrote *Das Kapital* and the *Communist Manifesto* in Soho, England.

And this clearly reveals that communism is not merely a so-called ideology; it is a secret weapon, designed to serve the purpose of the Illuminati.

Weishaupt died in 1830, but prior to his death, he prepared a revised version of the conspiracy, which under various aliases was to organize, finance, direct, and control all international organizations and groups by working their agents into executive positions at the top.

In the United States, we have Woodrow Wilson, Franklin Roosevelt, Jack Kennedy, Johnson, Rusk, McNamara, Fulbright, and both George Bushes as prime examples.

In addition, while Karl Marx was writing the *Communist Manifesto* under the direction of one group of Illuminists, Professor Carl Ritter of Frankfurt University was writing the antithesis under the direction of another group.

The idea was that those who direct the overall conspiracy could use the differences between the two so-called 'ideologies' to divide larger and larger numbers of the human race into opposing camps, so that they could be armed and then brainwashed into fighting and destroying each other – and particularly, to destroy all political and religious institutions.

The work Ritter started was continued after his death and completed by the German philosopher Freidrich Nietzsche, who founded the Nietzschean school of thought. This was

later developed into Fascism and then into Nazism, and was used to create two World Wars.

In 1834, the Italian revolutionary leader Guiseppe Mazzini was selected by the Illuminati to direct their revolutionary program throughout the world. He served in that capacity until he died in 1872. It was Mazzini who enticed an American general named Albert Pike into the Illuminati.

Pike was fascinated by the idea of a world government, and ultimately he became the head of this Luciferian conspiracy. Between 1859 and 1871 he developed a plan for three world wars and various revolutions throughout the world; these would take the conspiracy to its conclusion during the twentieth century.

Albert Pike

Again, I remind you that these conspirators were never concerned with immediate success. They operate with a long term view.

Guiseppe Mazzini

Pike did most of his work in his home in Little Rock, Arkansas. But a few years later, when the Illuminati's Lodges of the Grand Orient became suspect and were widely repudiated because of Mazzini's revolutionary activities in Europe, Pike created what he called the 'New and Reformed Palladian Rite'.

He set up three Supreme Councils; one in Charleston, South Carolina, one in

Rome, Italy, and a third in Berlin, Germany. He also had Mazzini establish 23 subordinate councils in strategic locations throughout the world, and these have been the secret headquarters of the world revolutionary movement ever since.

Long before Marconi invented the radio, the scientists in the Illuminati had found the means for Pike and the heads of his councils to communicate secretly. It was the discovery of that secret that enabled them to control how apparently arbitrary incidents, such as the assassination of an Austrian Prince in Serbia, could be developed into a war or a revolution.

Pike's plan was as simple as it has proved effective. It called for Communism, Nazism, Zionism and other international

movements to be organized and used to create three global world wars, and at least two major revolutions.

The first world war was to be fought so as to enable the Illuminati to destroy Czarism in Russia – as vowed by Rothschild after the Czar had torpedoed his scheme at the Congress in Vienna – and to transform Russia into a stronghold of atheistic communism.

The differences between the British and German Empires stirred up by agents of the Illuminati were to be used to create this war. After the war ended, communism was to be built up and used to destroy other governments and weaken religions.

World War II, when and if necessary, was to be fomented by using controversies between fascists and zionists. Here let it be noted that Hitler was financed by Krupp, the Warburgs, the Rothschilds, and other internationalist bankers and that the slaughter of the supposed six million Jews by Hitler did not bother the Jewish globalist bankers at all.

That slaughter was necessary in order to create worldwide

Adolf Hitler Was a Rothschild

This is the Same Family that Owns the U.S. Fed and Controls Our Politicians

Lionel Nathan Rothschild	Alois Hitler Lionel Nathan Rothschild's Son	Adolf Hitler Lionel Nathan Rothschild's Grandson	Evelyn De Rothschild Lionel Nathan Rothschild's Great Grandson

Matild Schueckelgruber, a servant at the Rothchild's mansion had an illegitimate son with Lionel Nathan Rothschild (22 Nov. 1808 –3 June 1879) named Alois Schueckelgruber (7 June 1837 –3 January 1903).
2)Alois Schueckelgruber married Ciara Poltzi (Alois officially changed his last name with the Austrian Minsistry to Hitler. Hitler was his mother in law's maiden name, he took it rather than carry his mother's name making him known to be illegitimate)
3)They had 3 children (Gustav, Adolf, and Paula)
4) Evelyn De Rothschild, Owner of the US Fed, is the Great Grandson of Lionel Nathan Rothschild. He is the Man Who Controls Our Politicians.

Why do We Have a DIRECT Relative to Adolf Hitler Controlling the U.S?

hatred of the German people, and thus bring about war against them. In short, this second World War was to be fought to destroy Nazism and increase the power of Zionism so that the state of Israel could be established in Palestine.

During this second World War, international Communism was to be built up until it equalled in strength united Christendom. When it reached that point; it was to be contained and kept in check until required for the final cataclysm.

As we know now, Roosevelt, Churchill, and Stalin put that

exact policy into effect and Truman, Eisenhower, Kennedy, Johnson, and George Bush all continued that exact same strategy.

World War III is to be fomented, using false flags and controversies, by the agents of the Illuminati operating under the many names by which plot is now known. They operate among the political Zionists and the leaders of the Muslim world.

That war is to be directed in such a manner that all of Islam and political Zionism will destroy each other while at the same time the remaining nations, once more divided on this issue, will be forced to fight themselves and each other into a state of complete exhaustion – physically, mentally, spiritually, and economically.

Now, can any thinking person doubt that the intrigue now

"**Military men are just dumb stupid animals, to be used as pawns in foreign policy.**"

– *Henry Kissinger*

going on in the Middle and Far East is designed to accomplish that very satanic objective?

Pike himself foretold all this in a statement he made to Mazzini on August 15, 1871. He wrote that after World War III is ended, those who aspire to undisputed world domination will provoke the greatest social cataclysm the world has ever known.

Quoting his own words taken from the letter he wrote to Mazzini (and the letter is now catalogued in the British Museum in London, England) he said the following:

"We shall unleash the nihilists and the atheists, and we shall provoke a great social cataclysm, which in all its horror will show clearly to all nations the effect of absolute atheism, the origins of savagery and bloody turmoil.

Then everywhere, the people will be forced to defend themselves against the world revolutionaries, and will exterminate those destroyers of civilization; and the multitudes disillusioned with Christianity, whose spirits will be from that moment without direction and leadership and anxious for an ideal – but without knowledge where to direct its adoration – will receive the true light through the universal manifestation of the pure doctrine of Lucifer, brought finally out into public view.

This will result from a general reactionary movement which will follow the destruction of Christianity and atheism; both of them conquered and exterminated at the same time."

When Mazzini died in 1872, Pike made another revolutionary leader named Adrian Lemmy his successor. Lemmy, in turn, was succeeded by Lenin and Trotsky, who were in turn followed by Stalin. The revolutionary activities of all those men were financed by British, French, German and American international bankers, all of them dominated by the House of Rothschild.

We are supposed to believe that the international bankers of today, like the money-changers of Christ's day, are only the tools or agents of the great conspiracy; but actually they are the masterminds behind all the mass media, promoting the deception that Communism is a movement of the so-called 'workers'.

The fact is that British and American intelligence officers have authentic documentary evidence proving that globalist liberals, operating through their banking houses – particularly the House of Rothschild – *have financed both sides of every war and revolution since 1776.*

Those who today comprise the conspiracy direct our governments – whom they hold in usury through such institutions as the Federal Reserve in America – to fight wars

"The real menace to our Republic is the invisible government which like a giant octopus sprawls its slimy legs over our cities, states and nation. At the head is a small group of banking houses generally referred to as 'international bankers'.

This little coterie run our government for their own selfish ends.

It operates under cover of a self-created screen and seizes our executive officers, legislative bodies, schools, courts, newspapers, and every agency created for the public protection."

John F. Hylan, 96th Mayor of New York City

such as Vietnam, so as to further Pike's plans to bring the world to that stage of the conspiracy when atheistic Communism and the whole of Christianity can be forced into an all-out world war within each remaining nation, as well as on an international scale.

The headquarters of the great conspiracy in the late 1700s was in Frankfurt, Germany, where the House of Rothschild had been established by Mayer Amschel, who adopted the Rothschild name and linked together other international financiers who had literally sold their souls to the Devil.

After the Bavarian government's exposure in 1786, the conspirators moved their headquarters to Switzerland, and then on to London.

Since World War II (after the death of Jacob Schiff, the Rothschild agent), their American headquarters have been in the Harold Pratt Building in New York City, and the Rockefellers, originally proteges of Schiff, have taken over the manipulation of finances in America for the Illuminati.

In the final phases of the conspiracy, the one-world government will consist of the king or dictator – the head of the United Nations – the CFR, and a few billionaires, economists, and scientists who have proved their devotion to the great conspiracy.

The rest of the population is to be integrated into a vast conglomeration of mongrelized humanity; literally slaves.

Now let me show you how our federal government and the American people have been sucked into the plans for a one-world state; and bear in mind that the United Nations was created to become the vehicle for that worldwide 'liberal' conspiracy.

The real foundations of the plot for the takeover of the

"I see in the near future a crisis approaching that unnerves me and causes me to tremble for the safety of my country.... corporations have been enthroned and an era of corruption in high places will follow, the money power of the country endeavors to prolong its reign by working upon the prejudices of the people, until all wealth is aggregated in a few hands, and the Republic is destroyed."

US President Abraham Lincoln
Nov 21, 1864

United States were laid during our Civil War. Not that Weishaupt and the earlier masterminds had ever overlooked the new world, as I have previously indicated; Weishaupt had his agents planted over here as far back as the Revolutionary War.

It was during the Civil War that the conspirators launched their first concrete efforts. We know that Judah Benjamin, chief advisor of Confederate President Jefferson Davis, was a Rothschild agent.

We also know that there were Rothschild agents planted in Abraham Lincoln's cabinet who tried to involve him in a financial deal with the House of Rothschild. But Lincoln saw through the scheme and rejected it, thereby incurring the undying enmity of the Rothschilds, just as the Russian Czar had when he torpedoed the first League of Nations, at the Congress of Vienna.

Investigation of Lincoln's assassination revealed that the assassin, Booth, was a member of a conspiratorial group. Because a number of highly important government officials were involved, the name of the group was never revealed and it became a mystery, just as the assassination of John

THESE ARE THE ONLY TWO PRESIDENTS WHO EVER ATTEMPTED TO END THE FEDERAL RESERVE BANKING SYSTEM

WHAT ELSE DO THEY HAVE IN COMMON???

F. Kennedy is still a mystery. (Although I am sure it will not remain a mystery forever.)

The ending of the Civil War removed for the moment any chance of the Rothschilds gaining control of the American financial system, as they had done in Britain and other nations in Europe.

But the Rothschild Illuminati never quit. They had to start from scratch, and they lost no time in getting started.

Shortly after the Civil War, a young Jacob Schiff arrived in New York. The son of a Rabbi born in one of the Rothschild's houses in Frankfurt, Germany, he was on a mission for the House of Rothschild.

The Rothschilds recognized in him Machiavellian qualities that could make him a valuable part of the one-world conspiracy.

After a comparatively brief training period in the Rothschilds' London bank, Jacob left for America, with instructions to buy into a banking house, which was to be the springboard to acquire control of the financial system of the United States.

Schiff had four specific assignments:

1. To acquire control of America's financial system.

2. To find men and women willing to serve as stooges for the great conspiracy, and promote them into high places in the federal government, the Congress, the U.S. Supreme Court, and all federal agencies.

3. To create strife throughout the nations between minority groups, particularly between the whites and blacks.

4. To create a movement to destroy religion in the United States, with Christianity being the chief target.

JACOB SCHIFF

The first and most important of these objectives was to get control of the United States' financial system.

As a first step, he had to buy into a banking house; but it had to be one that he could absolutely control, and mold for the primary objective of entrapping the American economy.

Schiff bought a partnership in the firm Kuhn and Loeb. Like Schiff, Kuhn and Loeb were immigrants from German Jewish ghettos. They came to the U.S. in the mid 1840s, and both of them started their business careers as itinerant peddlers.

In the early 1850s, they pooled their interests and set up a store in Lafayette, Indiana, servicing the covered wagons of the settlers on their way west. In the years that followed, they set up similar stores in Cincinnati and Saint Louis.

Then they added pawn-broking to their retail operations. From that to money-lending was a short and quick step.

By the time Schiff arrived on the scene, Kuhn and Loeb was a well-known private banking firm.

Shortly after he became a partner in Kuhn and Loeb, Schiff married Loeb's daughter Teresa. Then he bought out Kuhn's interests and moved the firm to New York, where it became Kuhn, Loeb, and Company, international bankers, with Schiff, agent of the Rothschilds, ostensibly the sole owner.

And throughout his career this blend of Judas and

Machiavelli, the first heirarch of the Illuminati's conspiracy in America, posed as a generous philanthropist and a man of great holiness; this was the cover-up devised by the Illuminati.

As I have stated, the first great step of the conspiracy was to be the entrapment of our economic system. To achieve that objective, Schiff had to get the full cooperation of the large banks in America; and that was easier said than done.

Even in those years, Wall Street was the heart of the American money-mart, and J.P. Morgan was its dictator. Next in line were the Drexels and the Biddles of Philadelphia. All the other financiers, big and little, danced to the music of those three houses; but particularly to that of Morgan. All of those three were proud, haughty and arrogant potentates.

For the first few years, they viewed the little bewhiskered man from the German ghettos with utter contempt; but Schiff knew how to overcome that. He threw a few Rothschild bones to them; the distribution in America of desirable European stock and bond issues.

Then he discovered that he had a still more potent weapon in his hands, in the following.

It was in the decades following the Civil War that American industries began to burgeon. We had great railroads to build. The oil, mining, steel, textile industries were bursting out of their swaddling clothes.

All of that required vast financing, and much of it had to come from abroad. Now Schiff came into his own, and he played a very crafty game. He became the patron saint of John D. Rockefeller, Edward R. Harriman, and Andrew Carnegie.

He financed the Standard Oil Company for Rockefeller, the railroad empire of Harriman, and Carnegie's steel empire.

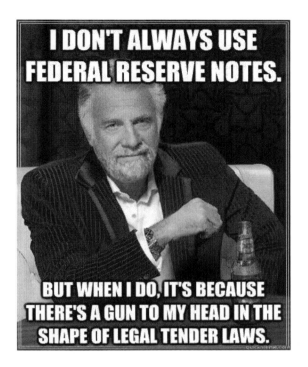

I DON'T ALWAYS USE FEDERAL RESERVE NOTES.

BUT WHEN I DO, IT'S BECAUSE THERE'S A GUN TO MY HEAD IN THE SHAPE OF LEGAL TENDER LAWS.

But instead of hogging all the other industries for Kuhn, Loeb and Company, he opened the doors of the House of Rothschild to Morgan, Biddle, and Drexel.

In turn, Rothschild arranged the setting up of branches in London, Paris, and other European cities for those three, always in partnerships with Rothschild subordinates.

Rothschild made it very clear to all those concerned that Schiff was to be the boss in New York.

By the turn of the century, Schiff had taken complete control of the entire banking sector of Wall Street – which by then, with Schiff's help, included the Lehman brothers, Goldman-Sachs, and other internationalist banks that where headed by men chosen by the Rothschilds.

With that control of the nation's banks, Schiff was then

ready to execute the next giant step – the entrapment of the entire American national money system.

Under our Constitution, control of the money system is vested solely in the Congress. Schiff's next step was to seduce our Congress to betray that Constitutional edict by surrendering that control to the hierarchy of the Illuminati's great conspiracy.

In order to legalize that surrender and thus make the people powerless to resist it, it would be necessary to have Congress enact special legislation.

To accomplish that, Schiff infiltrated stooges into both houses of Congress; stooges powerful enough to railroad Congress into passing such legislation.

Equally, or even more importantly, he had to plant a stooge in the White House – a President without integrity and without scruples who would sign the necessary legislation into law. To accomplish that, he had to take control of either the Republican or the Democratic Party.

The Democratic Party was the more vulnerable, as it was the hungrier of the two.

Except for Grover Cleveland, the Democrats had been unable to land one of their men in the White House since before the Civil War.

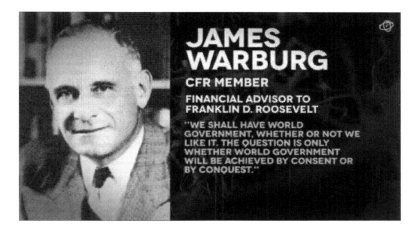

JAMES WARBURG

CFR MEMBER

FINANCIAL ADVISOR TO FRANKLIN D. ROOSEVELT

"WE SHALL HAVE WORLD GOVERNMENT, WHETHER OR NOT WE LIKE IT. THE QUESTION IS ONLY WHETHER WORLD GOVERNMENT WILL BE ACHIEVED BY CONSENT OR BY CONQUEST."

There were two reasons for that:

1. The poverty of the Democratic Party.
2. There were many more Republican-minded voters than Democrats.

The poverty matter was not a great problem, but the voter problem was a different story.

Here is the atrocious and murderous method he employed to solve that problem with the voters. His solution illustrates how little the Jewish internationalist bankers care about their own racial brethren.

Suddenly, around 1890, there broke out in Russia a nationwide series of pogroms. Many thousands of innocent Jewish men, women, and children were slaughtered by the Cossacks and other peasants. Similar pogroms with similar slaughter of innocents broke out in Poland, Rumania, and Bulgaria.

As a result of the violence, terrified Jewish refugees swarmed into the United States. The influx continued for two or three decades, as the pogroms were continuous through all those years. All this was fomented by Rothschild agents.

All those refugees were aided by self-styled 'humanitarian' committees set up by Schiff, the Rothschilds, and their affiliates.

At first most of the refugees streamed into New York, but the Schiff-Rothschild humanitarian committees found ways to shuffle many of them into other large cities such as Chicago, Boston, Philadelphia, Detroit and Los Angeles.

All of them were quickly naturalized as U.S. citizens and encouraged to register as Democrats. Thus the minority groups became solid Democratic voter blocks within their communities, all controlled and maneuvered by their so-called benefactors.

And shortly after the turn of the century; they became vital factors in the political life of our nation. That was one of the methods Schiff employed to plant men like Nelson Aldrich in our Senate and Woodrow Wilson in the White House.

At this point let me remind you of another one of the important jobs that was assigned to Schiff when he was dispatched to America. I refer to the job of destroying the unity of the American people by creating racial strife.

By the pogrom-driven Jewish refugees entering into America; Schiff was creating a ready-made minority-group for that purpose. But the Jewish people, as a whole, made fearful by the pogroms, could not be depended upon to create the violence necessary to destroy the unity of the American people.

Within America, there was an already made-to-order, although as yet sleeping minority group: the black population. The plan was to incite them into so-called 'demonstrations' – rioting, looting, murder, and every other type of lawlessness. All that was necessary was to arouse them.

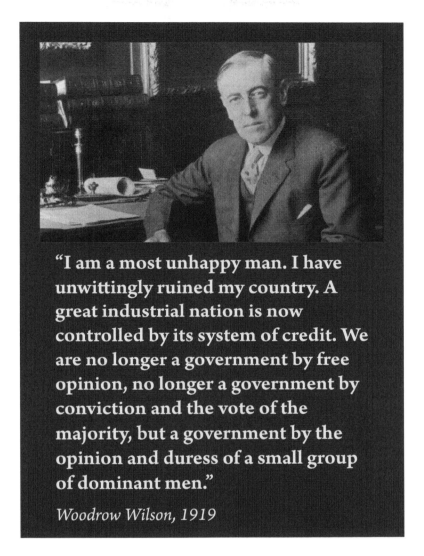

"I am a most unhappy man. I have unwittingly ruined my country. A great industrial nation is now controlled by its system of credit. We are no longer a government by free opinion, no longer a government by conviction and the vote of the majority, but a government by the opinion and duress of a small group of dominant men."

Woodrow Wilson, 1919

Together, those two minority groups, properly maneuvered, could be used to create exactly the strife and chaos in America that the Illuminati would need to accomplish their objective.

Thus while Schiff and his co-conspirators were laying their plans for the takeover of our financial system, they were also perfecting plans to hit the unsuspecting American people with an explosive and terrifying racial upheaval that would divide the population into hate-ridden factions.

"For the first time in its history, Western Civilization is in danger of being destroyed internally by a corrupt, criminal ruling cabal which is centered around the Rockefeller interests, which include elements from the Morgan, Brown, Rothschild, Du Pont, Harriman, Kuhn-Loeb, and other groupings as well. This junta took control of the political, financial, and cultural life of America in the first two decades of the twentieth century."

Carroll Quigley

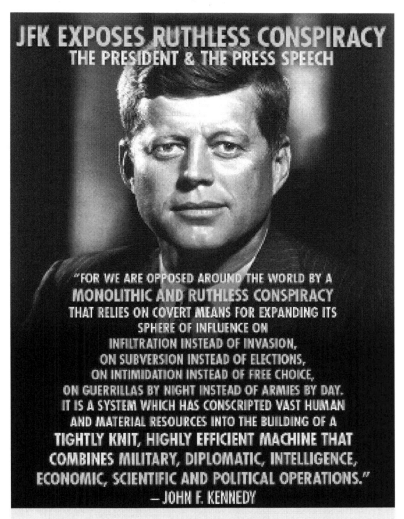

JFK EXPOSES RUTHLESS CONSPIRACY
THE PRESIDENT & THE PRESS SPEECH

"FOR WE ARE OPPOSED AROUND THE WORLD BY A
MONOLITHIC AND RUTHLESS CONSPIRACY
THAT RELIES ON COVERT MEANS FOR EXPANDING ITS
SPHERE OF INFLUENCE ON
INFILTRATION INSTEAD OF INVASION,
ON SUBVERSION INSTEAD OF ELECTIONS,
ON INTIMIDATION INSTEAD OF FREE CHOICE,
ON GUERRILLAS BY NIGHT INSTEAD OF ARMIES BY DAY.
IT IS A SYSTEM WHICH HAS CONSCRIPTED VAST HUMAN
AND MATERIAL RESOURCES INTO THE BUILDING OF A
**TIGHTLY KNIT, HIGHLY EFFICIENT MACHINE THAT
COMBINES MILITARY, DIPLOMATIC, INTELLIGENCE,
ECONOMIC, SCIENTIFIC AND POLITICAL OPERATIONS."**
— JOHN F. KENNEDY

JFK tried to inform the people of this Nation that the Office of the President of the United States was being manipulated by an elite. At the same time, he put a stop to the 'borrowing' of Federal Reserve Notes from the Federal Reserve Bank, and began issuing United States Notes (which was interest-free) on the credit of the United States. It was the issuing of the United States Notes that caused Jack Kennedy to be assassinated.

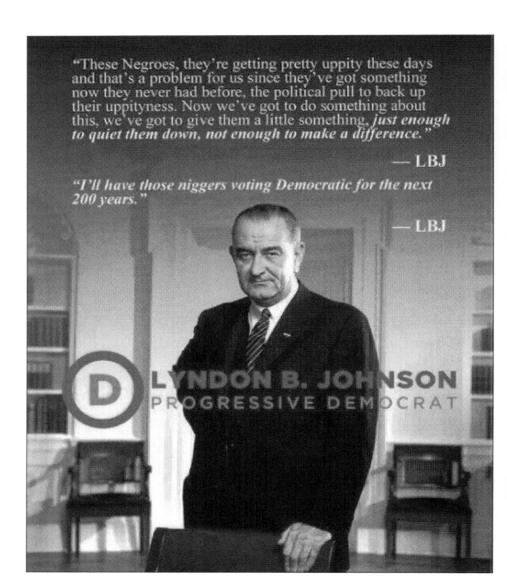

I tried to issue interest-free money into the system so the American people wouldn't be enslaved by the banking cartel. The Federal Reserve had me killed.

They would create chaos throughout the nation, especially on the college and university campuses – all protected by Earl Warren decisions and our so-called leaders in Washington D.C.

Of course, perfecting those plans required time and infinitely patient organizing.

On becoming President, Lyndon B. Johnson stopped the issuing of the United States Notes and went back to borrowing Federal Reserve Bank Notes (which at the time were loaned to the people of the United States at the going rate of interest of 17%). The U.S. Notes, that were issued under John F. Kennedy, were of the 1963 series which bore a red seal on the face.

Now, to remove all doubts, I'll take a few moments to give you some background to this plot to create racial strife.

First of all they had to create the leadership and organizations to draw in millions of Jews and blacks, who would do the demonstrating and commit the rioting, looting, and lawlessness.

So in 1909, Schiff, the Lehmans, and other conspirators set up the *National Association for the Advancement of the Colored People*, known as the NAACP. The presidents, directors, and legal councils of the NAACP were invariably white and appointed by Schiff. This remains the case to this very day.

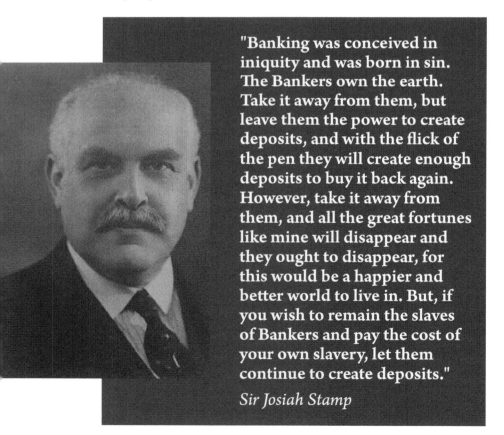

"Banking was conceived in iniquity and was born in sin. The Bankers own the earth. Take it away from them, but leave them the power to create deposits, and with the flick of the pen they will create enough deposits to buy it back again. However, take it away from them, and all the great fortunes like mine will disappear and they ought to disappear, for this would be a happier and better world to live in. But, if you wish to remain the slaves of Bankers and pay the cost of your own slavery, let them continue to create deposits."

Sir Josiah Stamp

RACHEL DOLEZAL

Then in 1913, the Schiff group organized the *Anti-defamation League of the B'nai B'rith* (commonly known as the ADL) to serve as the gestapo and hatchet-man for the entire great conspiracy.

Today the ADL maintains over two thousand agencies in all parts of our country, and they advise and completely control every action of the NAACP and the National Urban League of all the other so-called black civil rights organizations, including those of such leaders as Martin Luther King, Stockely Carmichael, and Barnard Rustin.

In addition, the ADL acquired control of the advertising budgets of many advertising agencies, department stores, hotel chains and television and radio sponsors, in order to control the mass media and force newspapers to slant and falsify the news; and to further incite – and at the same time create sympathy for – the lawlessness and violence of the mobs.

Here is documentary proof of the beginning of their plot to foment lawlessness.

THE MELTING POT

THE GREAT AMERICAN DRAMA

BY ISRAEL ZANGWILL

Around 1910, one Israel Zangwill wrote a play called *The Melting Pot*. It was propaganda, designed to incite violence. The play purportedly described how the American people were discriminating against and persecuting Jews and blacks. At that time, nobody seemed to realize that it was propaganda; it was that well written – but the propaganda was well concealed in the truly great entertainment in the play, and it was a big hit on Broadway.

Now in those years, the legendary Diamond Jim Brady used to throw a banquet at the famous Delmonico Restaurant

Diamond Jim Brady

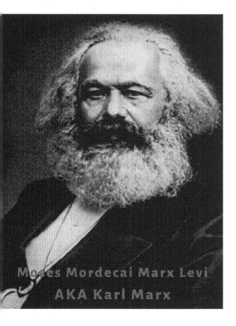

Moses Mordecai Marx Levi AKA Karl Marx

in New York after the opening performance of a popular play. He threw such a party for the cast of *The Melting Pot*, its author, producer, and other Broadway celebrities.

By then, I'd already made a mark on Broadway, and so I was invited to that party. There I met George Bernard Shaw and a Jewish writer named Israel Cohen.

Zangwill, Shaw, and Cohen were the ones who created the Fabian Society in England and had worked closely with a Frankfurt Jew named Mordicai who had changed his name to Karl Marx, but remember; at that time both Marxism and Communism were just emerging, and nobody paid them much attention, or noticed the propaganda in the work of those three brilliant writers.

At that banquet, Israel Cohen told me that he was engaged in writing a book which was to be a follow-up on Zangwill's *The Melting Pot*. The title of his book was to be *A Racial Program for the 20th Century*.

At that time I was completely absorbed in my work as a

ISRAEL COHEN

playwright – and as significant as that title was, its real objective never dawned on me; nor was I interested in reading the book. But its importance hit me with the force of a bomb when I received a newspaper clipping of an item published by the *Evening Star* newspaper in May 1957. That item was a verbatim reprint of the following excerpt from Cohen's *A Racial Program for the 20th Century*.

So the authenticity of the passage in Cohen's book was confirmed. However, the question that remained in my mind was whether it represented the official policy of the Communist Party, or just a personal expression of Cohen himself.

Hence I sought more proof – and I found it, in an official pamphlet published in 1935 by the New York Communist Party.

That pamphlet was entitled *The Negroes in a Soviet America*. It urged blacks to rise up, form a soviet state in the South, and apply for admission to the Soviet Union! It also contained a firm pledge that the revolt would be supported by all American communists, as well as so-called 'liberals'.

Now there's only one question, and that is to prove that the communist regime would be directly controlled by Jacob Schiff and the Rothschilds.

A little later, I will show that the Communist Party was created by the capitalists Schiff, the Warburgs, and the

"We must realize that our party's most powerful weapon is racial tension. By propounding into the consciousness of the dark races that for centuries they have been oppressed by the whites, we can move them to the program of the communist party.

In America; we will aim for subtle victory. While inflaming the Negro minority against the whites; we will instill in the whites a guilt-complex for their exploitation of the Negroes.

We will aid the Negroes to rise to prominence in every walk of life, in the professions, and in the world of sports and entertainment. With this prestige, the Negro will be able to intermarry with the whites and begin a process which will deliver America to our cause."

Representative Thomas G. Abernethy, Congressional record of June 7, 1957

Rothschilds, who had planned and financed the entire Russian Revolution, and the murder of the Czar and his family. Lenin, Trotsky, and Stalin all took their orders directly from Schiff and the other capitalists, whom they supposedly were fighting.

The Illuminati plan is to create tension and strife between blacks and whites.

Can you see why the Earl Warren issued his decision prohibiting Christian prayer and Christmas carols in our schools? And why Kennedy did likewise? And can you see why Johnson and 66 Senators, despite the protests of 90% of the American people, voted for the 'Consular Treaty' which opened our entire country to Russian spies and saboteurs? All those 66 Senators are twentieth century Benedict Arnolds.

It is up to you, the American people, to force Congress, our elected servants, to haul in those American traitors. There should be Congressional investigations of the CFR and all its fronts, such as the ADL and the NAACP.

Such investigations will unmask the traitors in Washington. They will also expose the United Nations as the crux of the plot, and force Congress to take the United States out of the U.N. and expel the U.N. itself from American territory.

HAS IT OCCURED TO ANYONE THAT IF YOU'RE ABLE TO ORGANIZE THIS MANY PEOPLE FOR A PROTEST

YOU CAN ORGANIZE THIS MANY PEOPLE TO CLEAN UP YOUR COMMUNITY AND GET RID OF THE CRIMINAL ELEMENT CAUSING THE PROBLEM?

Before we conclude this section, I wish to reiterate one vital point, which I urge you to never forget if you wish to save our country for your children, and for their children.

Here is the point. Every unconstitutional and unlawful act committed by Woodrow Wilson, Franklin Roosevelt, Truman, Eisenhower, Kennedy and Johnson, is exactly in keeping with the centuries-old plot outlined by Weishaupt and Albert Pike.

Every decision issued by the treacherous Earl Warren and his equally treacherous Supreme Court justices was directly in line with what the Illuminati blueprint required.

All the treason committed by our State Department under Rusk, and earlier by John Foster Dulles and Marshall, and all the treason committed by McNamara and his predecessors is directly in line with that same blueprint for the takeover of the world.

Now I will go back to Jacob Schiff's entrapment of our financial system, and the treasonous actions that followed. I

THE FEDERAL RESERVE BOARD, 1917

will also reveal the Schiff-Rothschild control of not only Karl Marx; but also of Lenin, Trotsky, and Stalin, who created the revolution in Russia and set up the Communist Party.

It was in 1908 that Schiff decided that the time had come to take control of America's financial system. His chief lieutenants in the exercise were Colonel Edward Mandell House, whose entire career was that of chief executive and courier for Schiff, as I shall show, as well as Bernard Baruch and Herbert Lehman.

In the autumn of that year, they assembled in a secret conclave at the Jeckle Island Hunt Club, owned by J.P. Morgan at Jeckle Island, in Georgia. Among those present were J.P. Morgan, John D. Rockefeller, Colonel House, Senator Nelson Aldrich, Schiff, Stillman and Vandlelip of the New York National City Bank, W. and J. Seligman, Eugene Myer, Bernard Baruch, Herbert Lehman, Paul Warburg – in short; all of the international bankers in America.

All of them were members of the conspiracy.

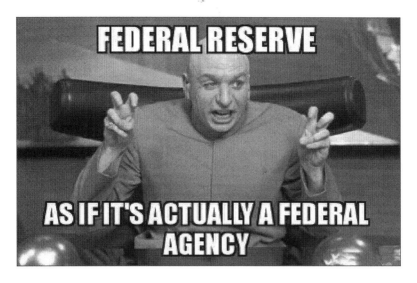

FEDERAL RESERVE

AS IF IT'S ACTUALLY A FEDERAL AGENCY

A week later, they emerged with what they called the *Federal Reserve*.

Senator Aldrich was the stooge who was to railroad it through Congress, but they delayed that for one chief reason; they would first have to plant their man and obedient stooge in the White House, to sign the *Federal Reserve Act* into law. They knew that even if the Senate would pass that act unanimously, the then newly-elected President Taft would promptly veto it.

So they waited.

In 1912, their man Woodrow Wilson was elected to the presidency.

Immediately after Wilson was inaugurated, Senator Aldrich railroaded the *Federal Reserve Act* through both houses of Congress, and Wilson promptly signed it. into law. That happened on December 23, 1913, two days before Christmas when all the members of Congress, except for several carefully picked Representatives and three equally carefully picked Senators, were away from Washington.

How heinous treasonous was that act?

I'll tell you. Our founding fathers knew full well the power

TO LEARN HOW THE FEDERAL RESERVE BANK WORKS

11. What if the Bank runs out of money?
Some players think the Bank is bankrupt if it runs out of money. The Bank never goes bankrupt. To continue playing, use slips of paper to keep track of each player's banking transactions – until the Bank has enough paper money to operate again. The banker may also issue "new" money on slips of ordinary paper.

REFER TO RULE #11 OF THE POPULAR BOARD GAME 'MONOPOLY'

of money. They knew that whoever had that power held the destiny of our nation in his hands.

That is why they said in the Constitution that Congress – the elected representatives of the people – alone would have the power. The language used in the Constitution on this point is brief, concise, and specific. Article I, Section 8, Paragraph 5 of the Constitution defines the duties and powers of Congress "to coin money, regulate the value thereof, and of foreign coin, and the standard of weights and measures."

Yet on that day of infamy, December 23, 1913, the men we sent to Washington to safeguard our interests – the Representatives, Senators, and President Woodrow Wilson – delivered the destiny of our nation into the hands of two aliens from Eastern Europe; Jacob Schiff and Paul Warburg. (Warburg was a recent immigrant, who came here on orders from Rothschild for the express purpose of blueprinting the *Federal Reserve Act.*)

Up until 1913 Americans kept all of their earnings. Despite this, we still had: schools, colleges, roads, vast railroads, streets, subways, the Army, Navy and the Marine Corps, (who managed to win 8 wars).

Tell me again why We The People need to be extorted ???

Now the vast majority of the American people think that the Federal Reserve System is a United States Government agency. That is absolutely false. All of the stock of the federal reserve banks is owned by the member banks, and the heads of the member banks are all members of the Council on Foreign Relations (CFR).

The details of that act of treason are far too long for this book, but the complete story is available in a book entitled *The Federal Reserve Conspiracy*, written by Eustace Mullins. In that book Mullins tells the entire story, and backs it up with unquestionable documentation. Every American should read it.

Now, if you think that those aliens and their by-accident-of-birth American co-conspirators would be content with just the control of our money system, you are in for another sad shock.

The Federal Reserve System gave the conspirators complete control of our money system, but it in no way touched the earnings of the people, because the Constitution positively forbids what is now known as the 20% withholding tax.

But the blueprint for one world-enslavement called for the confiscation of all private property and control of individual earnings. This – and Karl Marx stressed this feature in his own writings – was to be accomplished through a progressive, graduated income tax.

CREATES FEDERAL RESERVE, MAKES PAPER MON WORTH GOLD (FICTITIOUS WEALTH), STARTS PROGRESSIVE LIBERALISM, PROLONGS THE GREA DEPRESSION, AND IS A SOCIALIST DEMOCRAT

SEEN AS THE GREATES PRESIDENT IN HISTOR

As I have stated, such a tax could not lawfully be imposed upon the American people. It is succinctly and expressly forbidden by our Constitution. Thus, only an Amendment to the Constitution could give the federal government such powers.

Well, that too was not an insurmountable problem for our Machiavellian plotters. The same elected leaders in both houses of Congress and the same President Woodrow Wilson, who had signed the infamous *Federal Reserve Act* into law amended the Constitution to create the federal income tax, known as the 16th Amendment. Both are illegal under our Constitution.

In short, the same traitors signed both betrayals, the *Federal Reserve Act* and the 16th Amendment, into law. However, it seems that nobody realized that the 16th Amendment was set up to rob – and I do mean *rob* – the people of their earnings via the income tax.

The plotters didn't fully use the provision until World War II when that great 'humanitarian' Franklin Roosevelt applied a 20% withholding tax on all small wage earners, and up to 90% on higher incomes. Of course, he promised that it would be only for the duration of the war, but what was a promise to

"Some even believe we are part of a secret cabal working against the best interests of the united states, characterizing my family and me as 'internationalists', and of conspiring to build a more integrated global political and economic structure – one world, if you will. If that's the charge, I stand guilty, and I am proud of it."

David Rockefeller

the charlatan who in 1940, when he was running for his third term, proclaimed "I say, again and again and again, that I will never send American boys to fight on foreign soil."

Remember that he was making that statement even as he was already preparing to plunge us into World War II by enticing the Japanese into that sneak attack on Pearl Harbor, to furnish him with an excuse.

And before I forget, let me remind you that another charlatan named Woodrow Wilson used exactly that same campaign slogan in 1916. His slogan was "Re-elect the man who will keep your sons out of the war," – exactly the same formula, exactly the same promise, and exactly the same result.

Now, the 16th Amendment income tax trap was intended to confiscate and rob the earnings of the common herd; in

"We are grateful to the *Washington Post*, the *New York Times, Time* and other great publications whose directors have attended our meetings and respected their promises of discretion for almost 40 years. It would have been impossible for us to develop our plan for the world if we had been subjected to the lights of publicity during those years. But the world is now more sophisticated and prepared to march towards a world government. The supranational sovereignty of an intellectual elite and world bankers is surely preferable to the national auto-determination practiced in past centuries."

David Rockefeller at a Bilderberg meeting in 1991

other words, you and I. It was not meant to touch the huge incomes of the Rockefellers, the Carnegies, the Lehmans, and all the other conspirators.

So together with that 16th Amendment, they created what they called the 'tax-free foundations' that would enable the conspirators to transform their huge wealth into such so-called 'foundations' and avoid payment of virtually all income taxes. The excuse for it was that the earnings of those 'tax-free foundations' would be devoted to humanitarian philanthropy.

So we now have the several Rockefeller Foundations, the Carnegie and Dowman Fund, the Ford Foundation, the Mellon Foundation, and hundreds of similar 'tax-free foundations'.

And what kind of philanthropy do these foundations

Illuminati

An organisation which somehow controls all media on earth
yet can't deal with conspiracy theory videos on YouTube.

support? Well, they finance all the civil rights groups and conservation-movements that are creating all the chaos and rioting all over the country. They finance the Martin Luther Kings. The Ford Foundation finances the Center for the Study of Democratic Institutions in Santa Barbara, commonly referred to as Moscow West, and which is headed by Wonder Boy Hutchens, Walter Ruther, Erwin Cahnam and others of that ilk.

In short, the 'tax-free foundations' finance those who are working for the Illuminati's conspiracy. And what are the hundreds of billions of dollars they confiscate every year from the earnings of the common herd used for?

Well, for one thing, there is the 'foreign aid' gimmick, which gave billions to the communist Tito, plus gifts of hundreds of jet planes, many of which were turned over to Castro, plus the costs of training communist pilots so that they can better shoot down our own planes.

Plus billions to red Poland, billions to India, and billions to Sukarno; as well as billions to many other enemies of the United States.

That is what that the treasonous 16th Amendment has done to our nation and to the American people – to you and to me, to your children and their children.

Our CFR and Illuminati-controlled federal government can grant tax-free status to foundations and one-world fronts, such as the 'Fund for the Republic'.

But if you or a patriotic organization is too outspokenly pro-American, they can terrify and intimidate you by finding a misplaced comma in your income tax declaration, and by threatening you with penalties, fines, and even prison.

Future historians will wonder how the American people could have been so naive and stupid as to have permitted such audacious acts of treason as the *Federal Reserve Act* and the Sixteenth Amendment.

Well, they were not naïve, and they were not stupid. The answer is that they trusted the representatives they elected to safeguard our country and our people, and they didn't suspect either betrayal – until after they had been accomplished.

It was the Illuminati-controlled mass media that has kept – and is still keeping – our people naive and stupid and unaware of the treason being committed.

Now the big question is "when will the people wake up and do to our traitors of today what George Washington and our founding fathers would have done to Benedict Arnold?" (Actually, Benedict Arnold was a petty traitor compared to our present traitors in Washington D.C.)

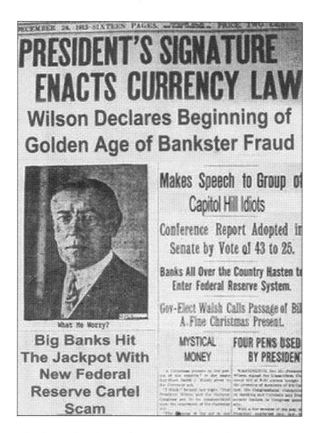

NOVEMBER 24, 1913 SIXTEEN PAGES. PRICE TWO CENTS

PRESIDENT'S SIGNATURE ENACTS CURRENCY LAW

Wilson Declares Beginning of Golden Age of Bankster Fraud

Makes Speech to Group of Capitol Hill Idiots

Conference Report Adopted in Senate by Vote of 43 to 25.

Banks All Over the Country Hasten to Enter Federal Reserve System.

Gov-Elect Walsh Calls Passage of Bill A Fine Christmas Present.

Big Banks Hit The Jackpot With New Federal Reserve Cartel Scam

What Me Worry?

MYSTICAL MONEY **FOUR PENS USED BY PRESIDENT**

Now, let's go back to the events that followed the rape of our Constitution by the passage of the *Federal Reserve Act* and the 16th Amendment.

Was Wilson completely under their control?

The masterminds of the great conspiracy put in motion their next – and what they hoped would be their final – steps to achieve their world government.

The first of those steps was to be World War I.

Why? The answer is simple. The only justification for a world government is that it will supposedly ensure peace. The only thing that can make people cry for peace is war. War brings chaos, destruction, exhaustion – to the winner as well as to the loser. It brings economic ruin to both.

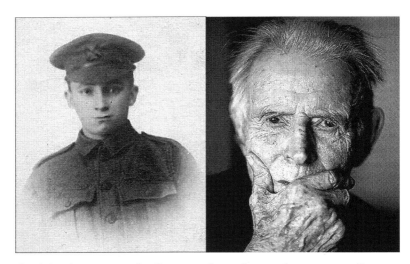

"I felt then, as I feel now, that the politicians who took us to war should have been given the guns and told to settle their differences themselves, instead of organizing nothing better than legalized mass murder. War is organized murder, and nothing else."

Harry Patch, the last surviving soldier of World War 1.

And most importantly, it destroys the flower of the young manhood of both. To the saddened and heartbroken mothers and fathers who are left with nothing but memories of their beloved sons, peace becomes worth any price.

That is the emotion upon which the conspirators depend for the success of their satanic plot.

Throughout the 19th century, from 1814 to 1914, the world, as a whole, was at peace. Such wars as the Franco-Prussian, our own Civil War, and the Russo-Japanese War, were what might be termed 'local disturbances' that did not affect the rest of the world.

All the great nations were prosperous, and the people were staunchly nationalistic and fiercely proud of their sovereignties. It was utterly unthinkable that the French and the German peoples would be willing to live under a one-world government; or the Turks, the Russians, the Chinese, or the Japanese.

Even more unthinkable is that a Kaiser Wilhelm or a Franz Joseph or a Czar Nicholas – or any monarch – would willingly and meekly surrender his throne to a world government.

But bear in mind that the peoples in all nations are the real power, and war is the only thing that can make the people yearn and clamour for peace – thus ensuring a world government.

But it would have to be a frightful and horribly devastating war. It could not be merely a local war between just two

nations; it would have to be a world war. No major nation must be left untouched by the horrors and devastation of such a war. The cry for peace must be universal.

The First World War was one of the bloodiest wars in all of history.

The British strategy during the Somme, for example, was that their soldiers were ordered to walk slowly towards the German machine guns and not to charge them or take cover, resulting in horrendous carnage. If they disobeyed, then they were placed in front of a firing squad of their own comrades – so, either way, death was certain.

Taking this as an example, it should be plain for you to see that the Illuminati have absolutely no qualms about slaughtering millions of people that they consider to be useless eaters, and neither will they have any qualms about slaughtering billions more, if necessary.

That was the approach used by the Illuminati and Nathan Rothschild from the turn of the 19th century onwards.

First they manoeuvred all of Europe into the Napoleonic Wars, and then into the Congress in Vienna which they – particularly Rothschild – planned to transform into a 'League of Nations' which was to have been the foundation of their one world system, exactly as the present United Nations is intended to be the framework for the forthcoming world government.

That was the approach that the Rothschilds and Jacob Schiff decided to employ to achieve their objective in 1914.

Of course, they knew that the same strategy had failed in 1814, but they theorized that this was only because the Czar of Russia had torpedoed that scheme; so the 1914 conspirators planned to remove that potential fly in the ointment.

They made sure that after the new world war they were planning, there would be no Czar of Russia around to ruin the plan.

Now, here is how to create a world war.

World War I was precipitated by a trivial incident. It was the kind of incident that both Weishaupt and Albert Pike had scripted; the assassination of an Austrian Archduke, arranged by the Illuminati masterminds.

War followed. It involved Germany, Austria, Hungary, and their allies – the so-called 'Axis powers' – against France, Britain, and Russia – the 'Allies'. Only the United States was not involved during the first two years.

By 1917 the conspirators had achieved their primary objective. Europe was in a state of destitution, and the population was war-weary and crying for peace. And the

outcome, too, was set.

The United States would soon be hurled into the war on the side of the Allies, and that was all set to happen immediately after Wilson's re-election. After that, there could be only one outcome – complete victory for the Allies.

When Wilson was campaigning for re-election in 1916, he asked the voters to "re-elect the man who will keep your sons out of the war."

But during that same campaign, the Republican Party publicly asserted that Wilson had long committed himself to commit the United States to the war. They charged that if he was defeated in the election, he would accomplish that act during his few remaining months in office; but if re-elected, he would hold off.

But at that time the American people looked upon Wilson as if he was some kind of god. He was duly re-elected, and in keeping with the intentions of the conspirators, in 1917 he took the United States into the war. He used the sinking of the Lusitania as the excuse – an incident which was prearranged.

Roosevelt – also a deity in the eyes of the American people – followed the same technique in 1941 when he used the prearranged Pearl Harbor attack as his excuse for taking us into World War II.

Now exactly as the conspirators planned, victory for the Allies eliminated the monarchs of the defeated nations and left their populations leaderless, confused, bewildered – perfectly conditioned for the world government that the conspiracy intended would follow.

But there still would be an obstacle – the same obstacle that had balked the Rothschilds at the Congress in Vienna after the Napoleonic Wars. Russia would be on the winning side, as it was in 1814, and therefore the Czar would still be securely on his throne.

Here it is pertinent to note that Russia, under the Czarist

regime, had been the one country in which the Illuminati had never made any headway, nor had the Rothschilds ever been able to infiltrate the Russian banking system; thus a victorious Czar would be more difficult than ever to deal with. Even if he could be enticed into a so-called 'League of Nations', it was a foregone conclusion that he would never agree to a one-world government.

So even before the outbreak of World War I, the conspirators had a plan to carry out Nathan Rothschild's 1814 vow to destroy the Czar – and also murder all possible heirs to the Russian throne.

It would have to be done before the close of the war, and the Russian Bolsheviks were to be their instruments.

From the turn of the century, the Bolshevik leaders were Vladimir Lenin, Leon Trotsky, and later Joseph Stalin. Of course, those were not their true family names prior to the outbreak of the Russian Revolution.

Trotsky's headquarters was on the lower East Side in New York, an area largely the habitat of Russian-Jewish refugees. Both Lenin and Trotsky lived well, yet neither had a regular occupation. Neither had any visible means of support, yet both always had plenty of money.

Those mysteries were solved in 1917.

Right from the outset of the First World War, strange and mysterious goings-on were taking place in New York. Night after night, Trotsky darted furtively in and out of Jacob Schiff's mansion.

In the dead of those same nights, there were gatherings of Russian refugees at Trotsky's headquarters in New York's lower East Side. They were going through some mysterious sort of training process that was shrouded in mystery. Nobody talked; although it did leak out that Schiff was financing all of Trotsky's activities.

Then suddenly Trotsky vanished, and so did approximately 300 of his trained thugs. Actually they were on the high seas in a ship chartered by Schiff, bound for a rendezvous with Lenin and his gang in Switzerland.

And also on that ship was twenty million dollars in gold. The money was to finance the Bolshevik takeover of Russia.

Cholly THE SMART SET
Knickerbocker

Who do you think financed Lenin, Stalin & Co. in Russia? The rich merchants and bankers of Russia, and those of Germany and the United States, of course. Old man Jacob Schiff, the New York banker, boasted that his money had been one of the causes of the first Russian Revolution of 1905.

Today it is estimated even by Jacob's grandson, John Schiff, a prominent member of New York Society, that the old man sank about $20,000,000 for the final triumph of Bolshevism in Russia. Ather New York banking firms also contributed.

In anticipation of Trotsky's arrival, Lenin prepared to throw a party in his Switzerland hideaway. Some of the most powerful people in the world were to be guests at that party.

Among them were Colonel Edward Mandell House, Woodrow Wilson's mentor and friend – but more importantly, he was Schiff's special and confidential messenger.

Another of the expected guests was Warburg of the Warburg banking clan in Germany, who was financing the

Kaiser, and whom the Kaiser had rewarded by making him chief of the secret police of Germany.

In addition; there were the Rothschilds from London and Paris, and also Lithenoth, Kakonavich, and Stalin (who was then the head of a gang of train and bank-robbing bandits).

And here I must remind you that England and France were by then well into their war with Germany, and that on February 3, 1917, Wilson had broken off diplomatic relations with Germany.

On account of the war in Europe Warburg, Colonel House, the Rothschilds and all those others were nominally enemies – but of course Switzerland was neutral ground where enemies could meet and be friends, especially if they had some scheme in common.

Lenin's little gathering was very nearly wrecked by an unforeseen incident. The ship that Schiff had chartered was intercepted on its way to Europe and taken into custody by a British warship. But Schiff quickly instructed Wilson to order the British to release the ship, intact with Trotsky's gang of 'revolutionaries', and of course the gold.

Wilson obeyed. He warned the British that if they refused to release the ship, the United States would not enter the war in April as he had promised a year earlier.

The British heeded the warning and did as they were told.

Trotsky arrived in Switzerland and the Lenin party went off as scheduled; but they still faced what ordinarily would have been the insurmountable obstacle of getting Lenin, Trotsky and their followers across the border into Russia.

That's where Warburg, the chief of the German secret police, came in. He loaded all the thugs into sealed freight cars and made all the necessary arrangements for their secret

entry into Russia.

The rest is history.

The revolution in Russia took place and all members of the royal Romanov family (*above*) were murdered.

My chief objective now is to show that communism, so-called, is an integral part of the Illuminati conspiracy for the enslavement of the world.

Communism is both their weapon and the bogeyman with which they terrify the peoples of the whole world. The conquest of Russia and the establishment of communism there was, in great part, organized by Schiff and the other international bankers right in our own city of New York.

A fantastic story?

Yes. Some might even refuse to believe it. For the benefit of any doubters: just a few years ago Charlie Knickerbocker,

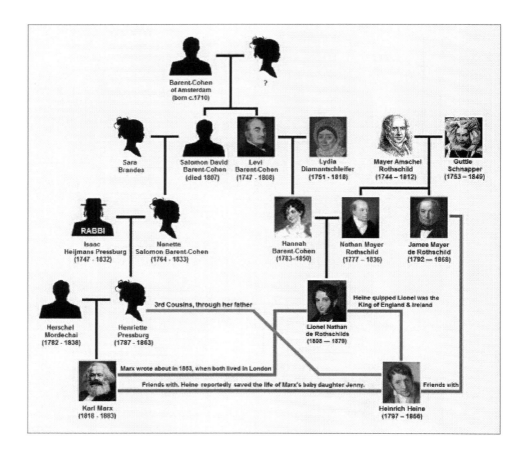

Barent-Cohen
of Amsterdam
(born c.1710)

?

Sara
Brandes

Salomon David
Barent-Cohen
(died 1807)

Levi
Barent-Cohen
(1747 - 1808)

Lydia
Diamantschleifer
(1751 - 1818)

Mayer Amschel
Rothschild
(1744 – 1812)

Guttle
Schnapper
(1753 – 1849)

Isaac
Heijmans Pressburg
(1747 - 1832)

RABBI

Nanette
Salomon Barent-Cohen
(1764 - 1833)

Hannah
Barent-Cohen
(1783–1850)

Nathan Mayer
Rothschild
(1777 – 1836)

James Mayer
de Rothschild
(1792 — 1868)

Herschel
Mordechai
(1782 - 1838)

Henriette
Pressburg
(1787 - 1863)

3rd Cousins, through her father

Lionel Nathan
de Rothschilds
(1808 — 1879)

Heine quipped Lionel was the
King of England & Ireland

Marx wrote about in 1853, when both lived in London

Friends with. Heine reportedly saved the life of Marx's baby daughter Jenny.

Karl Marx
(1818 - 1883)

Heinrich Heine
(1797 – 1856)

Friends with

a Hearst newspaper columnist, published an interview with John Schiff, grandson of Jacob, in which young Schiff confirmed the entire story, and named the exact figure that Jacob Schiff had contributed – twenty million dollars.

If anybody still has any doubt that the menace of communism was created by the masterminds of the great conspiracy here in our own city of New York, consider the following historical fact.

History shows that when Lenin and Trotsky engineered the capture of Russia, they acted as the leaders of the Bolshevik party. Now 'Bolshevik' is a Russian word, and the masterminds realized that 'Bolshevism' could never be sold as a brand or ideology to any but the Russian people.

So in April 1918, Jacob Schiff dispatched Colonel House to Moscow with orders to Lenin, Trotsky, and Stalin to change the name of their organization to the Communist Party, and to adopt Karl Marx's Communist Manifesto as the constitution of the Communist Party.

The Bolshevik leadership obeyed, and so in 1918 the Communist Party came into being. All this is confirmed in *Webster's Collegiate Dictionary*, Fifth Edition. In short: communism was created by the capitalists.

Until November 11, 1918 (the end of the war), the conspirators' fiendish plan worked perfectly. All the great nations, including the United States, were war-weary, devastated, and mourning their dead. Peace was universally desired.

Thus when President Wilson proposed the establishment of the League of Nations to 'ensure peace', all the great nations – without a Russian Czar to stand in their way – jumped onto that bandwagon, without pausing to read the fine print.

"From the days of Spartacus, Wieskhopf, Karl Marx, Trotsky, Rosa Luxemberg and Emma Goldman, this world conspiracy played a definite, recognizable role in the tragedy of the French Revolution. It has been the mainspring of every subversive movement during the 19th century.

And now, at last, this band of extraordinary Personalities from the underworld of the great cities of Europe and America have gripped the Russian people by the hair of their head and have become the undisputed masters of that enormous empire."

Winston Churchill

CENTRAL EUROPE IN 1914

Miles 400
Kilometers 640

NORWAY
SWEDEN
GREAT BRITAIN
DENMARK
RUSSIAN EMPIRE
NETH.
BELGIUM
LUX.
GERMANY
FRANCE
SWITZ.
AUSTRIA-HUNGARY
ITALY
Corsica
MONTE NEGRO
SERBIA
ROMANIA
BULGARIA
ALBANIA
OTTOMAN EMPIRE
Sardinia
Sicily
Algeria

CENTRAL EUROPE After World War I

States or regions created or reestablished by peace treaties.

NORWAY
SWEDEN
FINLAND
ESTONIA
GREAT BRITAIN
DENMARK
LATVIA
LITHUANIA
DANZIG
SOV. RUS.
GERMANY
NETH.
BELGIUM
LUX.
SAAR
GERMANY
POLAND
FRANCE
SWITZ.
CZECHOSLOVAKIA
AUSTRIA
HUNGARY
ROMANIA
ITALY
Corsica
YUGOSLAVIA
BULGARIA
ALBANIA
GREECE
Sardinia
Sicily
Algeria

All but one: the United States. The very nation that Schiff and his co-conspirators least expected to balk and let the side down was the one that refused to join.

When Schiff planted Wilson in the White House, the conspirators had assumed that they had the United States in the bag. Wilson had been built up as a great humanitarian, and was supposedly seen as a deity by the American people. There was every reason for the conspirators to believe that he would easily maneuver Congress into buying the idea of the League of Nations, sight-unseen, exactly as a later Congress of 1945 signed up for the United Nations, equally sight-unseen.

But there was one man in the Senate in 1918 who saw

through that scheme, just as the Russian Czar had in 1814. He was a man of political stature almost as great as that of Teddy Roosevelt, and fully as astute. He was highly respected and trusted by all members of both houses of Congress and by the American people. That great and patriotic American was Henry Cabot Lodge (not the phony who called himself Henry Cabot Lodge Jr., until he was exposed). Lodge completely unmasked Wilson, and kept the United States out of the League of Nations.

There is more to the real reason for Wilson's 'League of Nations' flop. As previously stated, Schiff was sent to the United States to carry out four specific assignments:

"I have loved but one flag, and I cannot share that devotion and give affection to the mongrel banner invented for the league of nations."

"True Americanism is opposed utterly to any political divisions resting on race and religion."

"We would not have our country's vigor exhausted or her moral force abated by everlasting meddling and muddling in every quarrel, great and small, which afflicts the world."

"Internationalism, illustrated by the Bolshevik and by the men to whom all countries are alike – provided they can make money out of them – is to me repulsive."

Henry Cabot Lodge

1. Most importantly – to take complete control of the U.S. money-system.

2. He was to find men to serve as stooges, and promote them into our Congress, the Supreme Court, and all the federal agencies such as the State Department, the Pentagon, the Treasury Department, etc.

3. He was to destroy the unity of the American people by creating strife between minority groups throughout the nation; especially between the whites and blacks, as outlined in Israel Cohen's book.

4. He was to create a movement to destroy religion in the United States, with Christianity to be the chief target.

In addition, he intended to gain control of the mass media, so as to brainwash the people into believing and accepting everything that the conspiracy required. Control of the press – at that time our only mass media – was necessary to destroy the unity of the American people.

Schiff and his fellow conspirators set up the NAACP (the National Association for the Advancement of the Colored People) in 1909, and in 1913 they established the ADL, or the 'Anti-Defamation League' of the B'nai B'rith.

Both were to be used to create the necessary strife, but in the early years, the ADL operated timidly – perhaps for fear of a pogrom-like action by an aroused and enraged American people. The NAACP was also largely dormant, because its white leadership hadn't realized that they would have to develop militant black leaders to spark racial unrest.

In addition, Schiff was busy infiltrating stooges into the government in Washington, into acquiring control of our money system and creating the 16th Amendment. Also, he was busy with organizing the plot for the takeover of Russia.

In short, he was kept so busy with all those jobs that he could not complete the task of acquiring control of our mass media.

That oversight was a direct cause of Wilson's failure to lure the United States into the League of Nations. When Wilson decided to go to the people to overcome the opposition of the Lodge-controlled Senate, despite his established (but phony) reputation as a great humanitarian, he found himself faced by a solidly united people and a loyal press whose ideology was Americanism and the American way of life.

William English Walling

Mary White Ovington

W.E.B. DuBois

NAACP FOUNDED 1909

Henry Moskowitz

Oswald Villard

Ida B. Wells

At that time, due to the ineptness and ineffectiveness of the ADL and the NAACP, there were no organized minority groups; no overpowering problems with black Americans, and no so-called 'antisemitic' problems with which to sway the people's thinking. There were no lefts, and there were no rights, nor any prejudices that could be exploited.

So Wilson's 'League of Nations' appeal fell on deaf ears.

And that was the end of Woodrow Wilson, the conspirators' great humanitarian. He quickly abandoned his crusade and returned to Washington, where he shortly died an imbecile, of syphilis. That was the end of the League of Nations as a means of creating a world government.

Of course that debacle was a terrible disappointment to the conspirators, but they were not finished. This enemy never quits. They simply decided to reorganize, and try from scratch again.

By this time Schiff was very old and slow. He knew it. He knew that the conspiracy needed a new younger and more

active leadership. So on his orders, Colonel House and Bernard Baruch organized and set up the *Council on Foreign Relations* – the new front under which the Illuminati would continue to function in the United States.

The hierarchy of the CFR – its officers and directors – was composed principally of descendants of the original Illuminati, many of whom had abandoned their old family names, and acquired new Americanized names. For one example, we have Dillon, who was Secretary of Treasury of the United States, whose original name was Laposky. Another example is Pauley, head of the CBS TV channel, whose true name is Palinsky.

The membership of the CFR is approximately 1,000 in number, and includes the heads of virtually every industrial empire in America – such as Blough (president of the U.S. Steel Corporation), Rockefeller (king of the oil industry), Henry Ford II, and so on. Plus, of course, all the international

"The drive of the Rockefellers and their allies is to create a one-world government combining supercapitalism and Communism under the same tent, all under their control. Do I mean a conspiracy?

Yes, I do. I am convinced there is such a plot, international in scope, generations old in planning, incredibly evil in intent."

– Rep. Larry P. MacDonald
killed on Korean Air Lines 007, 1983

bankers. The heads of many of the 'tax-free' foundations are also CFR members.

In short, all the men who provide the money and influence to elect the Presidents of the United States, the Congressmen, the Senators, and who decide the appointments of our various Secretaries of State, of the Treasury, of every important federal agency – are members of the CFR, and they are obedient members indeed.

Now just to confirm that fact, here are the names of some of the United States Presidents who have been members of the CFR: Franklin Roosevelt, Herbert Hoover, Dwight D. Eisenhower, Jack Kennedy, Nixon, and George Bush. Others who were considered for the presidency include Thomas E. Dewey, Adlai Stevenson, and Barry Goldwater.

Among the cabinet members of the various administrations, we have had John Foster Dulles, Allen Dulles, Cordell Hull, John J. MacLeod, Morganthau, Clarence Dillon, Rusk, McNamara – and just to emphasize the 'red' flavor of the CFR, we have seen as its members such individuals as Alger Hiss, Ralph Bunche, Pusvolsky, Harry Dexter White (real name Weiss), Owen Lattimore, and Phillip Jaffey.

Now, there were many jobs that the new CFR had to accomplish, and to achieve that, they needed help. So their first job was to set up various 'subsidiaries' to whom they assigned special tasks. They included the Foreign Policy Association (FPA), the World Affairs Council (WAC), the Business Advisory Council (BAC), Americans for Democratic Action (ADA), and the notorious '13-13' in Chicago.

In addition, the CFR set up special committees in every State in the Union to whom they assigned various operations.

Simultaneously, the Rothschilds set up similar groups in

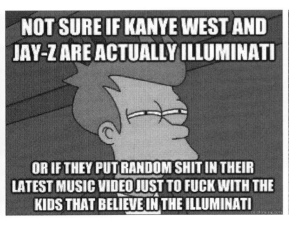

England, France, Germany, and other nations, with the intention of influencing world events and working with the CFR to bring about another world war.

But the CFR's first and foremost job was to take control of our mass media.

The control of the press was assigned to Rockefeller. Henry Luce was financed to set up a number of national magazines, among them *Life*, *Time*, and *Fortune*. The Rockefellers also directly or indirectly financed the Coles brothers' Look Magazine, and a chain of newspapers.

They also financed Sam Newhouse to buy up and build a chain of newspapers all over the country. And the late Eugene Myer, one of the founders of CFR, bought the *Washington Post*, *Newsweek*, the *Weekly Magazine*, and other publications.

At the same time, the CFR began to develop and nurture a new breed of columnists, editorialists, and writers such as Walter Lippman, Drew Pearson, the Alsops, Herbert Matthews, Erwin Canham, and others of that ilk who called themselves 'liberals' – who proclaimed that Americanism is

'isolationism', that isolationism is 'war mongering', that 'anti-communism' is 'anti-Semitic' and 'racist'.

All that took time, of course; but today our magazines and newspapers are completely controlled by CFR-aligned stooges. They have finally succeeded in breaking us up into a nation of quarreling, squabbling, hate-filled factions. If you still wonder about the slanted news and outright lies that you read in your newspaper, you now have the answer.

To the Lehmans, Goldman-Sachs, Kuhn-Loebs, and the Warburgs, the CFR gave the job of getting control of the motion picture industry, Hollywood, radio and television; and how they succeeded!

If you still wonder about the propaganda broadcast by the Ed Morrows and others of that ilk, you now have the answer. And if you wonder about all the smut and pornography that you see in your movie theater and on your television and which is derailing and demoralizing our youth so completely, you now have the answer.

Now, to refresh our memory, let's go back for a moment. Wilson's flop had torpedoed all possibility of transforming the League of Nations into the conspirators' world government. Jacob Schiff's plot had to be reset, to begin again

from scratch, and they organized the CFR to achieve that.

Also, we know how successfully the CFR did that job of brainwashing and destroying the unity of the American people.

But as was the case with the original Schiff plot, the creation of their global government would require yet another world war – one that would be even more horrible and more devastating than the first.

For the second time, the plan was to get the people of the world to clamor for peace, and to plead as one for an end to all wars.

But the CFR realized that the aftermath of World War II would have to be even more carefully planned, so that there could be no escape from the trap – a new League of Nations that would emerge in the aftermath.

That institution we now know as the United Nations, and they hit upon the perfect strategy to create it.

Here is how they did it.

In 1943, in the midst of the war, they prepared the framework for the UN, and it was handed over to Roosevelt and the State Department, to be delivered by Alger Hiss, Palvosky, Dalton, Trumbull, and other American traitors – thus making the whole scheme a United States' baby.

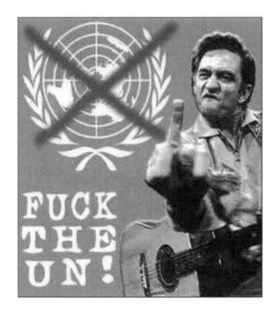

Then to confirm our parenthood, New York City was chosen to become the

> "Today Americans would be outraged if U.N. troops entered Los Angeles to restore order; tomorrow they will be grateful! This is especially true if they were told there was an outside threat from beyond, whether real or promulgated, that threatened our very existence. It is then that all peoples of the world will plead with world leaders to deliver them from this evil. The one thing every man fears is the unknown. when presented with this scenario, individual rights will be willingly relinquished for the guarantee of their well-being granted to them by their word government."
>
> *Henry Kissinger at a Bilderberger meeting in 1992*

nursery for this monstrosity. After that, the US could hardly walk out on its own baby, could it? Anyway, that's how the conspirators figured it would work, and so far it has. The Rockefellers donated the land for the United Nations building.

The UN charter was written by Alger Hiss, Palvosky, Dalton, Trumbull, and other CFR members. In 1945, a conference was convened in San Francisco. The representatives of over fifty nations gathered there and promptly signed the Charter. The traitor Alger Hiss flew to Washington with the document and with elation submitted it

to our Senate.

They signed it without so much as reading it, and with that the career of the United Nations began.

Since then, we have been repeatedly shocked, bewildered, and horrified by the UN's mistakes, for example in Berlin, Korea, Laos, Katanga, Cuba, and Vietnam. And their mistakes always favour the enemy, and never the United States.

Surely they should have made at least one or two mistakes in favor of the US, but they never do. Why is that?

The answer is the CFR, and the actions of their fronts and stooges in Washington. And complete control over our foreign policy is the key to the success of their plot.

The following is further proof.

Earlier, we saw that Schiff and his gang had financed the takeover of Russia by Lenin, Trotsky, and Stalin, and had fashioned its communist regime into becoming their main instrument to keep the world in turmoil, and to finally terrorize all of us into seeking peace and safety under a United Nations global government.

But the conspirators knew that the leadership in Moscow

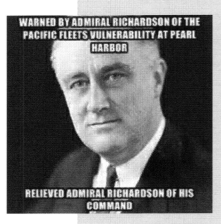

WARNED BY ADMIRAL RICHARDSON OF THE PACIFIC FLEETS VULNERABILITY AT PEARL HARBOR

RELIEVED ADMIRAL RICHARDSON OF HIS COMMAND

"For a long time, I felt that FDR had developed many thoughts and ideas that were his own to benefit this country, the USA. But he didn't. Most of his thoughts, his political 'ammunition', as it were, was carefully manufactured for him in advance by the CFR-One World money group. Brilliantly, with great gusto, like a fine piece of artillery, he exploded that prepared 'ammunition' in the middle of an unsuspecting target, the American people, and thus paid off and returned his internationalist political support.

The Depression was the calculated 'shearing' of the public by the World Money powers, triggered by the planned sudden shortage of supply of call money in the New York money market.... The One World Government leaders and their ever-close bankers have now acquired full control of the money and credit machinery of the U.S. via the creation of the privately owned Federal Reserve Bank."

Curtis Dall, FDR's son-in-law,
in his book My Exploited Father-in-Law

could not become the instrument they needed until the whole world accepted the communist regime as the legitimate government of Russia. Only one thing could accomplish that – diplomatic recognition by the United States.

They knew that the world would follow our lead and they

attempted to induce Presidents Harding, Coolidge, and Hoover to grant that recognition to the Soviet regime. But all three refused.

As a result, by the late 1920s, Stalin's regime in Moscow was in dire straits. Despite all the purges and the activities of the secret police, the Russian people were growing more and more resistive. It is a matter of record, admitted by Lipdenoff, that during 1931 and 1932, Stalin and his gang were always packed, and ready to flee the country at a moment's notice.

Then in November 1932, the conspirators achieved a great coup. They managed to install Franklin Roosevelt in the White House. That treacherous charlatan – crafty, unscrupulous, and absolutely without conscience – finally did the job for them. Without so much as asking for the consent of Congress, he unlawfully proclaimed recognition of Stalin's regime.

That did it. Exactly as the conspirators hoped, the world followed our lead. The Soviet regime was accepted. Any resistance among the Russian people was quickly crushed. And so was launched the greatest menace the civilized world has ever known. The rest is too well known to need repeating.

Roosevelt and his State Department kept building up and reinforcing the communist menace right here in our country, and thus throughout the world. He perpetuated the atrocity of Pearl Harbour, providing the excuse to hurl us into World War II.

He held secret meetings with Stalin at Yalta, and with Eisenhower's help delivered the Balkans and Berlin to Moscow.

And last, but by no means least, we know that this 20th century Benedict Arnold not only dragged us into the United Nations, but actually made all the arrangements to plant it within our country.

In short, the day that Roosevelt entered the White House, the CFR conspirators took control of our foreign relations, and firmly established the United Nations as the framework for a future world government.

There is one other important point. The Wilson 'League of Nations' flop led Schiff and his fellow conspirators to understand that control of just the Democratic Party alone was no longer enough.

Yes, they could create a crisis during a Republican administration, as they did in 1929 with the crash and subsequent depression which they manufactured through

the Federal Reserve, and which in all likelihood would bring another Democrat stooge back into the White House – but they realized that a four year disruption in their control of US foreign policy would play havoc with their scheme.

It could even disrupt their entire strategy, as it almost had before Roosevelt managed to save it with his recognition of Stalin's regime in Russia.

Thereupon, after that Wilson debacle, they began to formulate plans to achieve control of both of our national parties; but that posed a problem for them.

They needed manpower. They needed stooges in the Republican Party, as well as additional manpower in the Democratic Party. And control of the man in the White House alone would not be enough; they would have to provide their President with trained stooges, with which to stock his entire cabinet.

They would also need agents to head the State Department, the Treasury Department, the Pentagon, the CFR, the USIA, etc. In short, every member of both potential cabinets would have to be a chosen tool of the CFR, as well as all the under-Secretaries, assistant Secretaries, and other functionaries.

That would give the conspirators absolute control of all our policies, both domestic and, most importantly, foreign. That course of action would require a reserve pool of trained stooges, ready to instigate administrative changes as well as all

other exigencies. All such operatives would of necessity have to be people of national reputation, held in high esteem by the people – but they would also have to be men and women without honor, without scruple, and without conscience. And they would have to be vulnerable to blackmail.

It is unnecessary to stress how well the CFR succeeded. Senator Joe McCarthy revealed that there are thousands of such security risks to be found throughout the federal agencies. Scott MacLeod unmasked thousands more and you know the price that Ortega had to pay, and is still paying, for his expositions before a Senate Committee of the traitors in the State Department. We also know that the men in the State Department who delivered Cuba to Castro have not only been shielded, but promoted.

Now let's go back to the crux of the whole one-world government plot, and the maneuvering necessary to create another 'League of Nations' to house such a government.

As we have already seen, the conspirators knew that another

world war was central to the success of their plot. It would have to be such a horrifying and brutal war that the peoples of the world would cry out for the creation of some kind of a worldwide organization, to secure an everlasting peace.

But how could such a war be brought about? All the European nations were at peace. None had any quarrels with their neighboring nations, and certainly their agents in Moscow would not dare to start a war. Even Stalin realized that it would mean the overthrow of his regime – unless 'patriotism' could be used to weld the Russian people behind him.

But the conspirators had to have a war. They had to find – or create – some kind of an incident to launch it.

They found their proxy in an inconspicuous little man who called himself Adolf Hitler. Hitler, an impecunious Austrian house painter, had been a corporal in the German army. He took the defeat of Germany as a personal grievance, and began to 'rabble-rouse' about it in Munich.

He preached the restoration of the greatness of the German Empire, and the might of the German solidarity. He advocated the restoration of the German military. Strangely

"To achieve world government, it is necessary to remove from the minds of men their individualism, loyalty to family traditions, national patriotism, and religious dogmas."

Brock Chisholm, Director,
UN World Health Organization, 1991

enough, Hitler, the little clown that he was, could deliver a powerful rabble-rousing speech, and he did have a certain kind of magnetism.

But the new authorities in Germany didn't want any more wars, and they promptly threw the Austrian house painter into prison.

And here was the man, decided the conspirators, who if properly directed and financed could be the key to their world war.

So while he was in prison, they had Rudolph Hess and Hermann Goering write a book which they titled *Mein Kampf*. They attributed the book to Hitler, exactly as Lipdenoff wrote Mission to Moscow and then attributed the authorship to Joseph Davies, who was then our ambassador to Russia (and of course a CFR operative). And incidentally, *Mein Kampf* was actually a follow-up of Karl Marx's book *A World Without Jews*.

In *Mein Kampf*, the supposed author Hitler outlined his grievances, and how he would restore the German people to their former greatness. The conspirators then arranged for the wide circulation of the book among the German people, in order to arouse a fanatical following for him.

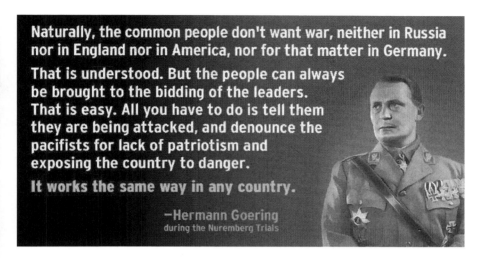

> Naturally, the common people don't want war, neither in Russia nor in England nor in America, nor for that matter in Germany.
>
> That is understood. But the people can always be brought to the bidding of the leaders. That is easy. All you have to do is tell them they are being attacked, and denounce the pacifists for lack of patriotism and exposing the country to danger.
>
> It works the same way in any country.
>
> —Hermann Goering
> during the Nuremberg Trials

On his release from prison (also arranged by the conspirators), they began to groom and finance him to travel to other parts of Germany to deliver his speeches and incite unrest. Soon he had gathered a growing following among other veterans of the war. His popularity soon spread to the masses, who began to see in him a saviour for their beloved Germany.

Then came his leadership of the 'brown-shirts', and the march on Berlin. That required a great deal of financing, but the Rothschilds, the Warburgs, and the other conspirators provided the money.

Hitler became an idol to the German people. The Nazis overthrew Von Hindenburg's government, and Hitler became the Fuhrer.

But still, that was no reason for a war. The rest of the world watched Hitler's rise, but saw no reason to interfere in what was distinctly a domestic process within Germany. Certainly, none of the other nations felt that there was sufficient reason for another war against Germany.

Also, the German people were not yet incited into enough

of a frenzy to commit any acts against any neighboring nation – not even against France – that would lead to a war.

The conspirators realized they would have to create a frenzy that would cause the German people to throw caution to the winds, and at the same time horrify the whole world.

The conspirators remembered how the Schiff-Rothschild gang had engineered the pogroms in Russia which slaughtered many thousands of Jews and created a worldwide hatred for Russia, and they decided to use that same unconscionable strategy to inflame the German people into a murderous hatred of the Jews.

Now, it is true that the German people never had any particular affection for the Jews, but neither did they have any particular hatred for them. Such a hatred would have to be manufactured; and Hitler was to create it.

This idea would have appealed to Hitler. He saw in it the grisly strategy that could make him the saviour of the German people.

There is a huge amount of literature describing how the Zionists made it very difficult to save Jews during and after World War II. As various individuals and organizations were trying to arrange departures of Jews to western countries, the Zionists worked overtime to prevent this from happening. They expressed the opinion that building up the Jewish population of Palestine was more important than enabling Jews to go to third countries, and they insisted to western powers that Jews should not be accepted anywhere other than Palestine. Indeed, Yitzhak Gruenbaum, a famous Zionist, proclaimed that "one cow in Palestine was worth more than all the Jews in Poland." The infamous David Ben-Gurion said in 1938:

"If I knew it was possible to save all the children in Germany by taking them to England, and only half of the children by taking them to Eretz Israel, I would choose the second solution. For we must take into account not only the lives of these children but also the history of the people of Israel."

And so, inspired and coached by his financial backers (the Warburgs, the Rothschilds, and all the other Illuminati masterminds) he blamed the Jews for both the universally hated Versailles Treaty and the financial ruin that beset Germany after the war.

The rest is history.

Here, let us reiterate how little the Jewish internationalist bankers – the Rothschilds, the Schiffs, Lehmans, Warburgs, and Baruchs – cared about their fellow Jews who were the victims of their nefarious schemes.

In their eyes, the slaughter of innocent Jews (or anyone else, for that matter) didn't bother them at all. They considered it a sacrifice that was necessary to further their plan for a world government, just as the slaughter of the many millions in the wars that followed was a necessary sacrifice.

And here is another grisly detail about those concentration camps. Many of the soldiers and executioners in those camps had previously been sent to Russia to refine their skills in torture and brutalization so as to emphasize the horrors of the atrocities.

All this created a new worldwide hatred for the German people, but it still did not provide sufficient cause for the required war. So Hitler was incited to demand the

Sudetenland, and we all remember how Chamberlain, along with Czechoslovakia and France, surrendered it up.

That success led Hitler to demand territories in Poland and in the French Ruhr, but those demands were rejected.

Then came his pact with Stalin. Hitler had been proclaiming his hatred of communism, but Nazism was actually National Socialism; and communism is, in fact, an international socialism. They are two variants of the same thing.

But Hitler disregarded all that. He entered into a pact with Stalin to attack and divide Poland between them. While Stalin marched into one half of Poland (for which he was never blamed; the historians have managed to forget that), Hitler launched his *blitzkrieg* on Poland from the German side.

The conspirators finally had their new world war – and what a horrible war it was.

And so in 1945, after six years of slaughter, the conspirators were finally able to achieve their United Nations, the vehicle for their world government.

And the American people hailed this unholy outfit. Even after all the facts about how the U.N. was created were revealed, the American people continued to support it.

Even after Alger Hiss was unmasked as a Soviet spy, the American people continued to accept the United Nations. Even after I had publicly revealed the secret agreement between Hiss and Mulatoff – that a Russian would always be the head of the military-secretariat and by that token, the real

OPERATION PAPERCLIP

THE NAZIS DIDN'T LOSE...

...THEY MOVED TO AMERICA

WERNHER VON BRAUN
NAZI / NASA ASSOCIATE ADMIN.

ARTHUR RUDOLPH
NAZI / NASA ROCKET SCIENTIST

HERMANN OBERTH
NAZI / NASA ROCKET SCIENTIST

From 1945 to 1955, Operation Paperclip granted nearly 1,000 German scientists American citizenship. Many had been longtime members of the Nazi party and the Gestapo and had conducted experiments on humans at concentration camps and committed other war crimes. The scientists ended up in the U.S. military industrial complex, worked with the CIA, NASA & more. One of the Nazi experiments that continued in America was mind control... known as the CIA's Project MK-ULTRA.

master of the United Nations.

But most of the American people continued to believe that the U.N. could do no wrong, even after Trygve Lie, the first Secretary-General of the U.N., confirmed the Hiss-Mulatoff agreement in his book *For The Cause of Peace*.

Vasialia was given a leave of absence by the U.N. so that he could take command of the North Koreans and Red Chinese who were fighting the U.N. 'police action' led by our own General McArthur (who on the orders of the U.N. was fired by the pusillanimous president Truman, in order to prevent him from winning that war.)

And the American people still believed in the U.N., despite our 150,000 sons who were murdered and maimed in Korea.

Did you know that the U.N. Charter was written by Alger Hiss, Mulatoff, and Vyshinsky? Or that Hiss and Mulatoff had made sure that the military chief of the U.N. was always to be a Russian, appointed by Moscow?

Did you know that at their secret meetings at Yalta, Roosevelt and Stalin, at the behest of the Illuminati operating as the CFR, decided that the U.N. must be placed on American soil?

Did you know that most of the U.N. Charter was copied intact, word for word, from Marx's *Manifesto* and the Soviet Russian constitution?

Did you know that the two senators who voted against the U.N. Charter were the only ones who had actually read it?

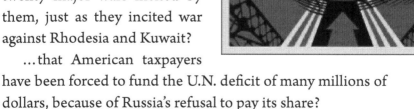

…that since the U.N. was founded, the number of people enslaved by communism has grown from 250 million to one billion?

…that since the U.N. was founded (supposedly to insure peace), there have been at least twenty major wars incited by them, just as they incited war against Rhodesia and Kuwait?

…that American taxpayers have been forced to fund the U.N. deficit of many millions of dollars, because of Russia's refusal to pay its share?

…that the U.N. had never passed a resolution condemning Russia or her so-called satellites, but always condemns our allies?

…that J. Edgar Hoover said: "the overwhelming majority

of the communist delegations to the U.N. are spies", and that 66 American senators voted for a 'Consular Treaty' to open our entire country to Russian spies and saboteurs?

…that the U.N. aids in the communist conquest of the world by preventing the free world from taking any action whatsoever, except to debate each new aggression in the U.N. General Assembly?

…that at the time of the Korean War, there were sixty nations in the United Nations; yet 95% of the U.N. forces were American soldiers, and practically 100% of the cost was paid by the United States?

…that the U.N. policy during the Korean and Vietnam Wars was to prevent us from winning those wars?

…that all the battle plans of General McArthur had to go first to the U.N. to be relayed to Vasialia, Commander of the North Koreans and Red Chinese?

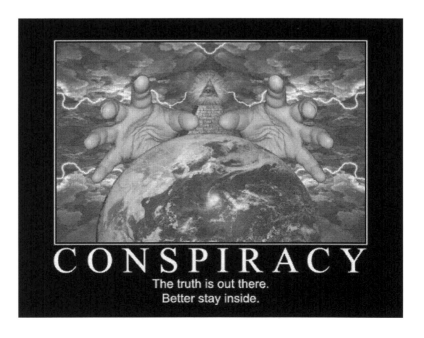

CONSPIRACY
The truth is out there.
Better stay inside.

THE UNITED NATIONS:

PROUDLY SERVING SATAN SINCE 1945

...that any future wars fought by our sons under the U.N. flag would have to be fought by our sons under the control of the U.N. Security Council?

...that the U.N. has never done anything about the 80,000 Russian Mongolian troops that occupy Hungary?

...where was the U.N. when Hungarian freedom fighters were slaughtered by the Russians?

...did you know that the U.N. and its 'peacekeepers' turned the Congo over to the communists?

...that the U.N.'s own so-called 'peace force' was used to crush, rape, and kill white anti-communists in Katanga?

...the U.N. stood by and did nothing while Red China invaded Laos and Vietnam?

...that it did nothing while Nero invaded Goa?

...that the U.N. was directly responsible for aiding Castro? That it does absolutely nothing about the many thousands of Cuban youngsters who are shipped to Russia for communist-indoctrination?

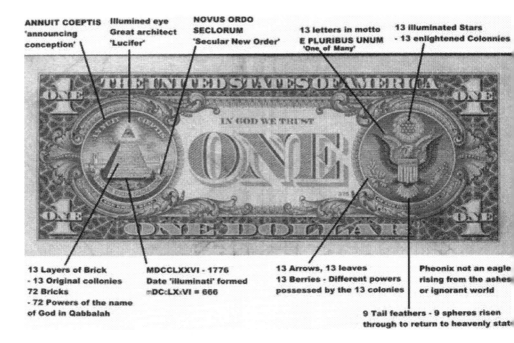

ANNUIT COEPTIS
'announcing
conception'

Illumined eye
Great architect
'Lucifer'

NOVUS ORDO
SECLORUM
'Secular New Order'

13 letters in motto
E PLURIBUS UNUM
'One of Many'

13 illuminated Stars
- 13 enlightened Colonnies

13 Layers of Brick
- 13 Original collonies
72 Bricks
- 72 Powers of the name
of God in Qabbalah

MDCCLXXVI - 1776
Date 'illuminati' formed
mDCcLXxVI = 666

13 Arrows, 13 leaves
13 Berries - Different powers
possessed by the 13 colonies

Pheonix not an eagle
rising from the ashes
or ignorant world

9 Tail feathers - 9 spheres risen
through to return to heavenly state

...that Adlai Stevenson said "the free world must expect to lose more and more decisions in the U.N."

...that the U.N. openly proclaims that its chief objective is a world government, which means 'one-world laws', 'one-world court', 'one-world schools', and a 'one-world church' in which Christianity would be prohibited?

...that a U.N. law has been passed to disarm all American citizens and to transfer all our armed forces to the U.N.? Such a law was secretly signed by 'saint' Jack Kennedy in 1961. Do you realize how that fits in with Article 47, paragraph 3, of the U.N. Charter, which states: "the military staff committee of the U.N. shall be responsible through the Security Council

for the strategic direction of all armed forces placed at the disposal of the Security Council."

...that when and if all our armed forces are transferred to the U.N., your children will be forced to serve and die under U.N. command all over the world. This will happen unless we get the U.S. out of the U.N.

...that Congressman James Utt has submitted a bill to get the U.S. out of the U.N., as well as a resolution to prevent our President from forcing us to support the U.N. embargoes on Rhodesia? Many people all over the country are writing to their representatives to support him.

Fifty Congressmen, spearheaded by Schweiker and Moorhead of Pennsylvania, have introduced a bill to transfer all our armed forces to the U.N. Can you imagine such brazen treason? Is your Congressman one of those fifty traitors? Find out and take immediate action against him and help Congressman Utt.

The National Council of Churches passed a resolution in

San Francisco which urges the United States to subordinate its will to that of the U.N., and that all American citizens must be prepared to accept it. Is your church a member of the National Council of Churches?

Bear in mind that God is never mentioned in the U.N. Charter and their meetings are never opened with prayer. The creators of the U.N. stipulated in advance that there should be no mention of God or Jesus Christ in their Charter, nor in the U.N. headquarters. The U.N. is a completely godless organization, and this is by orders of its creators, the CFR Illuminati.

By now you may have heard enough about the Illuminati and the United Nations.

There is one more message that needs to be understood.

One of the four assignments given to Jacob Schiff by Rothschild was to create a movement to destroy religion in the United States, with Christianity as the chief target.

The Anti-Defamation League (ADL) could not do it, because such an attempt could possibly create a terrible bloodbath; not only for the ADL and their fellow conspirators, but also for innocent Jews.

So Schiff turned the job over to the Baptist John D. Rockefeller for a specific reason; the destruction of Christianity could be accomplished only by those who are entrusted to preserve it; by the pastors; the men of the cloth.

As a starter, Rockefeller picked up a young (and so-called Christian) minister by the name of Harry Ward. At that time he was teaching religion at the Union Theological Seminary.

Rockefeller had found a willing Judas in this reverend, and in 1907, he financed his protege to set up the Methodist Foundation of Social Service.

Ward's job was to teach young men to become ministers, and to install them as pastors of churches. While teaching them to become ministers, Reverend Ward also taught them to preach to their congregations that the entire story of Christ was a myth, to cast doubts on the divinity of Christ and the Virgin Mary – in short, to cast doubts on Christianity as a whole.

It was not to be a direct attack. Much of it was to be done

through manipulation of the youth in the Sunday schools. Remember what Lenin's said: "Give me just one generation of youth and I'll transform the whole world."

Then in 1908, the Methodist Foundation of Social Service (which incidentally was America's first communist front), changed its name to the Federal Council of Churches.

But by 1950, the Federal Council of Churches was attracting too much suspicion, and so they changed their name to the National Council of Churches.

Do I need to tell you more about how the National Council of Churches is deliberately destroying faith in Christianity?

If you are a member of any congregation whose pastor and church are members of this Judas organization, you and your contributions are assisting the plot to destroy Christianity. You are delivering your children to be indoctrinated with disbelief in God and Church, and you will see them transformed into atheists.

Find out immediately whether your Church is a member of the National Council of Churches. And for the love of God and your children, if it is, withdraw from it.

However, let me warn you that the same process of destroying religion has been infiltrated into other denominations. You might have seen the black protests led and encouraged by ministers (including Catholic priests and nuns) who march with them. Yes, there are many individual churches and pastors who are honest and sincere; find one for yourself and for your children. (All you really have to know is whether your church is a 501(c)3 arm of the state. If it is, you should immediately stop attending it, and stop supporting it with your tax-deductible donations.)

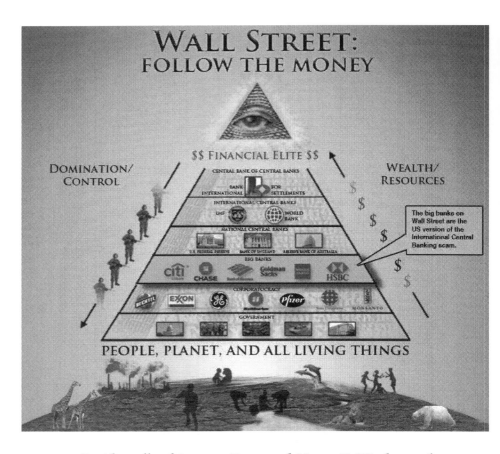

WALL STREET:
FOLLOW THE MONEY

PEOPLE, PLANET, AND ALL LIVING THINGS

Incidentally, this same Reverend Harry F. Ward was also one of the founders of the American Civil Liberties Union, a notoriously pro-Communist organization. He was the head of it from 1920 to 1940. He also was a co-founder of the American League against War and Fascism, which, under Browder, became the Communist Party of the United States.

In short, Ward's entire background reeked of communism and he was a member of the Communist party. He died a vicious traitor to both his church and country and this was the man John D. Rockefeller picked and financed to destroy America's Christian religion in accordance with the orders given to Schiff by the Rothschilds.

In conclusion, you probably are familiar with the story of how Dr. Frankenstein created a monster to destroy his victims, but how instead, the monster turned on its creator and destroyed him.

Similarly, the Illuminati/CFR created a monster called the United Nations, which was created to enslave and subjugate the people. We know all about that many-headed monster, and we know the names of those who created that monster.

I predict that one fine day the people of the world will wake, and cause that very monster to destroy its creator.

But for now, the majority of the population are still being brainwashed, deceived, and deluded by a traitorous press, TV, and radio, and by globalist traitors in the world's governments.

So, what will it take to rouse the people, and awaken them to the full proof? Enough books, articles and films will do it.

And I pray that this book will inspire you, all of you, to learn more, to study, and to spread this story to all loyal patriots in every country in the world.

Knowledge is the weapon with which we can destroy the monster. For the love of God, of your country, and of your children, use it.

David Spangler, Director of Planetary Initiative, United Nations

"Lucifer comes to give to us the final gift of wholeness. If we accept it then he is free and we are free. This is the Luciferic Initiation. It is one that many people now, and in the days ahead, will be facing, for it is an initiation in the New Age."

AND THIS
IS NOT EVEN
MY FINAL FORM

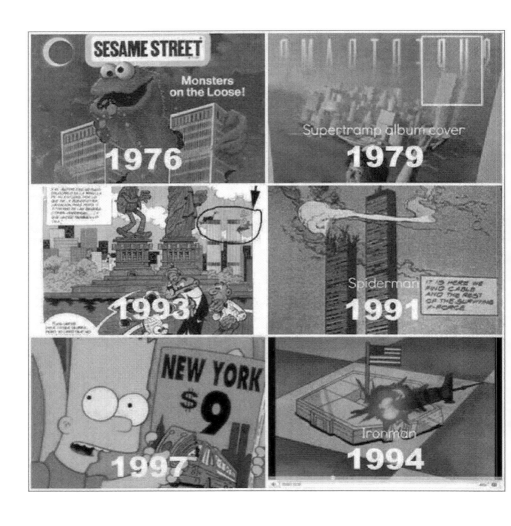

ADISTANTMIRROR.COM